T0128157

BETTER NEGOTIATING

JUTTA PORTNER

BETTER
NEGOTIATING

YOUR TRAINING BOOK FOR
BUSINESS AND PRIVATE LIFE

GABAL global
English Editions by GABAL Publishing

iUniverse®

BETTER NEGOTIATING
YOUR TRAINING BOOK FOR BUSINESS AND PRIVATE LIFE

First published by GABAL Verlag, Offenbach "Besser verhandeln. Das Trainingsbuch", 4ᵗʰ edition 2015.

Translated from German by Alex Gabriel.

iUniverse books may be ordered through booksellers or by contacting:

iUniverse
1663 Liberty Drive
Bloomington, IN 47403
www.iuniverse.com
1-800-Authors (1-800-288-4677)

ISBN: 978-1-5320-1367-6 (sc)
ISBN: 978-1-5320-1368-3 (e)

Library of Congress Control Number: 2017901721

Print information available on the last page.

iUniverse rev. date: 03/09/2017

CONTENTS

Dedicated to Jannic, Julien and Justin

JUST ONE WORD

What is the most important success factor of your negotiation? Within the last years I have asked participants of my negotiation trainings to express their experience in a single word. The result is a colorful collection of ideas. Please feel inspired and free to add whatever you like.

Activity. Action Steps. Active Listening. Affiliation. Alternatives. Appreciation. Attention. Autonomy. BATNA. Beliefs. Beyond Reason. Brainstorming. Capability of Showing Expression. Clarity. Commitment. Communication. Contact. Cooperation. Credibility. Courage. Creativity. Culture. Deepness. Direction. Discipline. Empathy. Engagement. Enjoying Experimenting. Exchange. Feedback. Flexibility. Focus. Fun. Fruitful Results. Getting To Yes. Getting Past No. Honesty. Humor. Information. Intensity. Interests. Joint Satisfaction. Joint Problemsolving. Mission. Motivation. Mutual Gain. Leadership. Liability. Objectives. Objective Criteria. Openness. Out of the Box. Overture. Partnership. Passion for Success. Playing. Persistency. Persuasion. Players. Power. Psychology. Questions. Rapport. Relax. Reliability. Respect. Rules. Seriousness. Sincerity. Spirit. Status. Strategies. Surprise. Sustainability. Tactics. Teamwork. Team spirit. Thinking. Time. Tricks. Trust. Values. Will to Change. Win-Win.

If you like to know more about the background of these single words and how to better negotiate in your next workshop, the upcoming family conference, a future meeting with customers or suppliers, allow yourself some quiet idle hours to read this book. That's all you have to do.

Have a good time and that reading will lead to a light bulb moment.

Jutta Portner & the team of C-TO:BE | THE COACHING COMPANY

1. LEARNING HOW TO BETTER NEGOTIATE

What is negotiation really all about?

When was the last time you negotiated? Was it while making weekend plans this morning with your significant other? Was it with your teenage son about some new tech gadget he says he needs? With your boss about a long-overdue salary raise? With a colleague who wants to leave for vacation at the same time as you? With some difficult, demanding client who keeps coming up with even more unreasonable requirements?

Negotiation is a part of our daily lives. It's something we do every single day. But do you usually think through beforehand how you will negotiate? No? That's okay – the same is true for most people. We normally just wing it in our day-to-day negotiations, simply going with our intuition instead of planning things out.

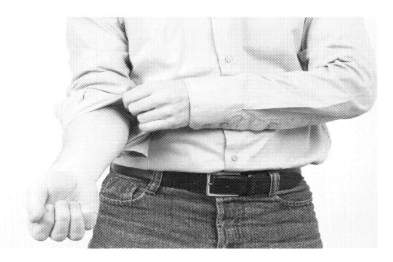

After reading this book,

- o you will understand the fundamentals and principles of both cooperative negotiation and competitive negotiation, as well as the differences between them,
- o you will have reflected upon – and improved – your own personal negotiating behavior, and
- o you will be able to professionally deal with difficult negotiating partners and unfair tactics.

This is a training book – which is what differentiates it from the conventional literature on the topic of negotiation. Most chapters begin with a self-assessment, through which you can evaluate your initial knowledge about the particular chapter's subject matter. The solutions for each self-assessment can be found at the end of the chapter. Case studies have also been included for each of the main topics dealt within this book; these "negotiation simulations" give you a chance to practice what you have learned. Additionally, the deep background information provided throughout the book enables you to acquire a more profound understanding of the subject matter.

SELF-ASSESSMENT 1.1

Neil Reubens has recently met a girl named Nellie. They have gone out a few times, and he really likes her. He will be taking her to the opera tonight; afterwards, he would like to invite her for a glass of wine at his place. The wine has been bought already, but now Neil needs a docking station for his iPhone. He is at the electronics store, where he has found an interesting, stylish model.

SALESMAN: This is a very elegantly designed system – the S-AIR iPhone docking station with built-in radio and two satellite speakers. You've picked a really nice model there. It'll be $589.

NEIL: That's pretty expensive. What kind of discount is available?

SALESMAN: Actually, the price of this system has already been reduced – it usually costs $70 more. You're really getting a bargain on this model – you're going to love it.

NEIL: I bought a washing machine and a stove from your store a month ago. I think a reasonable discount is in order.

SALESMAN: Unfortunately, I can't help you. As a matter of principle, we don't negotiate our prices. *(points to a corresponding sign on the wall)*

NEIL: I can't believe it! Listen, you can give me a good deal on this docking station – or would you rather I just go order it online?

SALESMAN: No, no, don't misunderstand me – of course I want to sell you this docking station. It's just that we generally don't offer extra discounts. I'm sorry.

▶ HOW WOULD YOU EVALUATE NEIL'S BEHAVIOR?

- I would've done exactly the same!
- Persistence usually pays off.
- Neil could have handled this better.

Read the expert opinion at the end of this chapter.

It is always amazing how negotiations tend to be approached so thoughtlessly and unstrategically. Each of the following is common practice among people while negotiating:

o Mistaking traditional marketplace haggling for actual negotiation.
o Thinking only about what they are negotiating for, while ignoring their relationships with their negotiating partners.
o Thinking that the negotiation has failed whenever they reach an impasse.
o Thinking that they are being persistent when they are actually just being stubborn.
o Feeling like they are "giving in" when they are working towards solutions with their counterparts.
o Picking up on other people's faults, while being blind to the flaws in their own negotiating style.
o Not recognizing dirty tricks and manipulation by other parties – and often being helpless even when they do recognize such tactics.
o Seeing moving slowly as a sign of weakness.
o Having no idea about how their facial expressions and body language are affecting the outcome of their negotiation.

We are often left frustrated by the results of negotiating by intuition alone. Emotions run high and we say or do things for which we will later be sorry. We damage our relationships with our negotiating partners. We get short-changed or ripped off. We end up with unsustainable results – and sooner or later need to negotiate all over again.

The Harvard Method

Thus, it is more effective to negotiate rationally, rather than just intuitively. To think before acting – and to think before reacting. With this in mind, researchers from Harvard University developed a pragmatic method, commonly known as the "Harvard Method", which strives to be a model for rational negotiation. The Harvard Method has been tried and tested many times over the years. It first appeared in the 1981 book *Getting to Yes: Negotiating an Agreement Without Giving In*, by Roger Fisher, William Ury, and later Bruce Patton, which is now the standard reference work on the topic of sound, rational negotiation. The bestseller has been translated into more than 20 languages around the world and has sold more than two million copies.

THE HARVARD NEGOTIATION PROJECT

The Harvard Negotiation Project is a research project devoted to the study of all aspects of negotiation. It is part of the Program on Negotiation (PON), a consortium affiliated with Harvard Law School, which includes faculty and projects from Harvard, MIT, and Tufts University's Fletcher School of Law and Diplomacy. It acts in four areas:

- *Theory building* – PON develops theories and models, such as the one now known and trademarked as the Harvard Method.
- *Education and training* – The project offers programs and courses for people (including diplomats, labor leaders, lawyers, and government officials) who work professionally with conflict resolution, negotiation, and mediation.
- *Publications* – The Teaching Negotiation Resource Center, formerly known as the PON Clearinghouse, offers a variety of materials including checklists, case studies, role-play simulations, videos, and books for teaching and training purposes.
- *Action research* – Current crisis hot-spots are professionally monitored, and conflict resolution support is offered to the involved parties as desired.

The philosophy behind the Harvard Method

How can results be reached even in difficult negotiations without either party losing face? Under what conditions can a fair agreement be reached between parties with opposite stances? In 1979, an interdisciplinary research team led by Roger Fisher, William Ury, and Bruce Patton dedicated itself to these key questions. The resulting "Harvard Method" is less a theory and more a practical approach for working towards a proper, mutually beneficial negotiation result. We are all familiar with the idea of striving for a "win-win situation" – in this case, we are speaking of cooperative negotiation.

Why negotiate in accordance with the Harvard Method?

If you successfully work with your counterpart towards a result that satisfies both of you, then you have truly won. And if you successfully use this result to lay a foundation for long-term, trusting cooperation, then you have gained even more. The Harvard Method serves as a tried and tested guide towards this end.

"The Harvard Method sharpens one's awareness of the negotiation process. This 'expansion of consciousness' is an important first step towards strengthening one's negotiation skills. It helps negotiating parties open their eyes... The method's approach to risks and uncertainties shows how anyone, whether a novice or an old hand, can negotiate in a sound, people-oriented manner." (Ulrich Egger, negotiation consultant, in the foreword to the German edition of *Getting to Yes*)

When can we speak of a "negotiation"?

Before continuing with this book about negotiation, let us first clarify a few basic concepts: What exactly constitutes a "negotiation"? Is every meeting or conversation automatically a negotiation as well? How can negotiating success be measured? What are the worst mistakes that can one can make while negotiating?

In this book, we speak about "negotiation" in the classical sense of the word – when individuals or other parties with divergent interests communicate with each other in order to reach an agreement.

The necessary conditions include:

o   Mutually dependent parties
o   A conflict of interest
o   An approximately equal balance of power
o   Agreement considered to be the goal of the negotiation

CASE STUDY: SPEEDY GONZALES

Carlos Gonzales' reputation precedes him – he is known as a tough negotiator. Carlos is the new purchasing manager for a large automobile company and has scheduled a negotiation meeting with an important, though financially distressed, supplier. The goal of the meeting is to negotiate the terms for a large contract. The supplier has had a close business relationship with the automobile company for many years; Carlos has called the supplier to meet him at his home. After the guests have been waiting for 20 minutes, Señor Gonzales appears – with a check in his hand. He pulls out his Montblanc pen, writes a number on the check, and places it face-down on the table. He looks directly at his counterpart and says, "You have until tomorrow morning to decide whether or not you are going to accept our offer." He then turns around and leaves the room, quietly and confidently.

▶ EXERCISE

Think about whether the situation described involves a negotiation, according to our definition of the word.

▶ ANALYSIS

Analyzing this situation, you can quickly determine that it clearly does not describe a negotiation in the classical sense of the word.

Regarding the first condition, we lack sufficient information to figure out whether the parties here are mutually dependent. We do not know whether the supplier has other customers, nor whether Señor Gonzales has other potential suppliers.

As for the question of a conflict of interest, this can be answered with a definite "yes". Both sides clearly have something that the other wants (the products / the order).

However, the balance of power here clearly is *not* equal. The purchasing manager for a large automobile company is in a much more powerful position than a financially distressed supplier. Carlos Gonzales uses this position of power to his advantage. It's a classic case of "take it or leave it" – there is one party dictating the terms here, rather than a mutual give-and-take for the benefit of both parties.

There does seem to be a desire to reach an agreement – otherwise, the two parties would not have shown up at the meeting.

Based on this case study, we can ultimately conclude that not every conversation between parties with conflicting interests is necessarily a true negotiation.

How can we measure the success of a negotiation?

The factors that determine whether or not a negotiation has been successful will be demonstrated below.

CASE STUDY: SKIING IN VERMONT

You live in Boston. It's a sunny Saturday in the middle of February, and there are eight inches of fresh powdery snow on the ground. An avid skier, you spontaneously decide to take your girlfriend to spend the day skiing in Vermont. It's a bit late, but half a day will be enough. You reach the ski resort at exactly noon. The chart at the counter says that a day pass is valid from 8am-5pm and costs $36, while a half-day pass is valid from 1-5pm and costs $21. Suddenly, you are approached by another skier, who asks whether you would like to buy his transferable day pass.

▶ EXERCISE

Play out the negotiation for the purchase of the day pass, either by yourself or with an actual conversation partner. What is the result of your negotiation? Are you satisfied with this result? Is the other skier also satisfied with the result? What criteria are you using to evaluate the result of your negotiation?

▶ ANALYSIS

- Do you care about getting an extra hour of skiing from noon to one o'clock?
- Are you concerned with each and every dollar that you can save off the price of the half-day pass?
- Is it important for you to get out on the slopes as soon as possible, thus making it worthwhile for you to pay even more than the price of the half-day pass?

- Are you so charmed by the seller that you end up going to grab a bite with him, the price of the pass being of secondary importance?
- Do you try to calculate the best solution mathematically, based on the cost per hour of skiing?

There is no *single* correct solution – rather just a perfect result for *you*.

The quality of a negotiation can be measured by:

o its effectiveness (quality of the result)
o its efficiency (based on the time invested)
o the negotiation climate (quality of the relationship)

A good negotiation result is:

o clear – without ambiguities
o feasible – no building castles in the air
o fair – no one is getting ripped off
o beneficial for both parties – based on the win-win principle
o sustainable – supported by both parties

In one-off negotiations – such as the purchase of the ski pass in the case study – price will be more important than your relationship with your negotiating partner. However, in most professional situations, you will want to be sure not to burn any bridges. If you will be engaging in long or frequent negotiations with someone, then it is worthwhile to adopt a cooperative negotiation style and proceed according to the Harvard Method.

We will examine both the cooperative and competitive negotiation styles in this book. Both are encountered in real life – and a good negotiator will have mastered both.

SELF-ASSESSMENT 1.2

Nellie Nelson has been invited to the opera. Now she just needs the perfect shoes to match her gorgeous evening gown. At the trendiest shop in the city, she finds exactly what she is seeking – a pair of silver high-heeled sandals. The price is $240. Nellie has already exhausted her budget with the purchase of her evening gown – so now she will have to negotiate!

NELLIE: I really love these shoes. I'm sorry, but might it be possible to get a small discount on the price?

...

NELLIE: These shoes are great. For $180 I'll take them!

...

NELLIE: Your prices are completely outrageous. Give me a reasonable price or I'll just go buy from someplace cheaper.

...

NELLIE: I'm going to need new winter boots next month – how much of a discount can you give me if I buy both pairs now?

▶ HOW WOULD YOU INITIATE THE NEGOTIATION IF YOU WERE IN NELLIE'S PLACE?

Read the expert opinion at the end of the chapter.

The biggest mistakes that can be made while negotiating

Interestingly enough, there are certain familiar elements that commonly lead to the failure of negotiations. You undoubtedly must have experienced failed negotiations at some point in your life. In the following practical exercise, check off the items that you recognize:

- **Pressure exerted on the weaker party**
  When one of the parties is in a stronger position than the others, he will tend to consciously or subconsciously exploit this fact.

- **Lack of flexibility**
  When situations change, negotiating parties often have difficulty adapting.

- **Tenacity**
  The more dependent a negotiating party is upon achieving his objective, the more likely it is that he will respond rashly or aggressively; this only hinders the development of a good game plan between parties who meet on equal terms.

- **Escalation**
  Pressure leads to counterpressure, which results in a spiral of escalation that the negotiating parties are often unable to escape on their own.

- **Compliancy**
  A fear of conflict often makes negotiators too defensive and submissive, and they end up making concessions without getting anything in return.

- **Inadequate preparation**
  The strategic effort exerted is often not commensurate with the value of the goal being pursued.

The three dimensions of negotiation

The concept of "3D negotiation" was coined by David A. Lax and James K. Sebenius. Lax was an investment banker before joining the Harvard Business School; he and Sebenius now run LaxSebenius LLC, a consulting firm specialized in negotiation strategy. Twenty years of negotiating experience went into the development of their 3D negotiation approach.

According to the 3D model, effective negotiation has three dimensions. Successful negotiators put lots of effort into the third dimension – which is often ignored by traditional negotiation courses. LaxSebenius LLC's extensive experience consulting on mergers and acquisitions, pharmaceutical deals, diplomatic negotiations, and labor negotiations has underscored the 3D approach's effectiveness.

The three dimensions are:

o Negotiating at the table – the actual negotiation process
o Negotiating on the drawing board – crafting the substance of the negotiation
o Pre-negotiation moves – setting up the scope of the negotiation

The first dimension

When most people think of negotiation, they think of the actual negotiation process. Aspects such as communication, behavior, body language, and negotiating tactics play important roles here. Information about these topics can be found in chapters 2, 3, and 4 of this book – they are definitely part of negotiation. However, they represent only one of the three dimensions. Such aspects actually have *less* influence on the final outcome than do the other two dimensions described below. Even experienced negotiators are often well-trained with regard to this first dimension, but weaker in the other two.

The second dimension

Many books on the topic of negotiation promote an appropriate preparation, instructing negotiators to develop creative solutions from which both sides benefit in the end. We take a closer look at this helpful tools in chapter 2, providing specific guidelines rather than just general advice. These guidelines will enable negotiators to develop an approach that cost themselves little, yet have great value both sides.

The third dimension

Improving the chances of a successful negotiation often means improving the framework conditions or expanding the scope for action – even before the actual negotiation takes place. You can thus make the solutions that you propose look more attractive to your counterparts than their alternative of walking away. Beyond the interactive process (first dimension) and the preparation of the negotiation (second dimension), this third dimension involves getting the right people to the table, at the right time, to negotiate the right issues, and demonstrating the right consequences of walking away if no deal is made. This dimension is the most strategic of the three, and highly successful negotiators invest much more energy in it. Information regarding this third dimension will be presented in chapter 2.

Dimension	Key aspects	Location	Focus	Goals
First dimension	Strategy and tactics	"at the table"	On the participants and the process	Improve negotiation technique, build trust, respond to unfair tactics
Second dimension	Preliminary deal design	"on the drawing board"	On values, substance, and results	Develop mutually beneficial compromises and sustainable solutions
Third dimension	Detailed pre-negotiation planning	"away from the table"	On the big picture	Increase scope for action as much as possible, carry out preliminary discussions

A recent example: Barack Obama lays the groundwork for health care reform

President Obama's plan for health care reform followed the 3D negotiation approach. Although we don't know whether the President has personally read Lax and Sebenius' book, the authorities who developed the reform package are certainly familiar with the concept. On June 17, 2009, I received the following email from Harvard's Program on Negotiation:

"The first secret of '3-D Negotiation' is to set the table—that is, create the right conditions for success before you ever sit down to negotiate. The President spent months 'setting the table'—inviting every conceivable interested party to the discussion, then filling the air with everyone-can-agree ideas like automating health record data and improving efforts at preventive care.

Next, proceed in the right sequence. After bringing the parties to the table and putting them in a good mood, the President threw the ball to Congress. Congress did what Congress does; it tossed the ball back and forth while the President looked from on high, nodding the occasional smile of approval.

*We're currently approaching the end-stage of a classic 3-D Negotiation, where the negotiator makes sure the discussion is focused on the right issues **and the right set of interests**. Thus, the President goes before the American Medical Association, a key interest group, and says he's now more open to controlling medical malpractice lawsuits … as long as doctors support his overall plan.*

Will the President follow our 3-D strategy to the endgame? Here's how to tell: He'll make sure he's negotiating at the right table—**the place where his desired outcome can occur—Congress, for example … and that he's ready to change tables if things go off track—perhaps sidestepping Congress via televised 'fireside chats' to the American people. The President will know the** *consequences* **of walking away from a deal he can't buy—and other parties will know that his threat to walk away is not a bluff."**

SOLUTIONS TO THE SELF-ASSESSMENTS

▶ SELF-ASSESSMENT 1.1

SALESMAN:....

NEIL: That's pretty expensive. What kind of discount is available? ("That's pretty expensive" is a deft remark – it makes it seem like Neil is still thinking about whether he actually wants to buy the docking station or not. Neil openly asks about a discount – that's okay. He also could have requested a specific discount amount.

SALESMAN:....

NEIL: I bought a washing machine and a stove from your store a month ago. I think a reasonable discount is in order. (Neil makes reference to previous purchases, thus putting pressure on the salesman to give him a discount in order to keep him as a loyal, high-value customer.)

SALESMAN: ...

NEIL: I can't believe it! Listen, you can give me a good deal on this docking station – or would you rather I just go order it online? (The salesman, who unfortunately is being a stickler, is getting on Neil's nerves. If Neil had been paying attention, then he would have realized that he was not dealing with the right partner for negotiation as soon as the salesman pointed at the sign. Neil thus feels compelled to take things up another notch, threatening to buy the device online. Unfortunately, it doesn't work.)

SALESMAN: ...

▶ SELF-ASSESSMENT 1.2

Answer 1:
Nellie proceeds very tentatively here. She makes it obvious that she wants to buy the shoes, then sheepishly asks about a discount. The salesman will just reply, "Sorry, I can't give you a discount", and Nellie will probably end up buying the shoes anyway. Right from the start, she's not firm enough.

Answer 2:
Nellie responds very forcefully here. She clearly states her price. The risk is that there might be little or no room for negotiation here. Nellie needs to think in advance about what she can do to keep her credibility intact in the event that the salesman doesn't go along.

Answer 3:
Nellie exaggerates impudently here ("completely outrageous"). She also supplements her verbal assault with a threat. The salesman will probably just react emotionally, saying "Then go buy your shoes somewhere else – I don't need to listen to you speak to me in that tone!"

Answer 4:
Nellie reacts rationally here. She knows that the shop will also benefit if she buys two pairs of shoes. She thus gives them a greater incentive to offer her a discount. Both sides will benefit here – the negotiations can begin.

SUMMARY: LEARNING HOW TO BETTER NEGOTIATE

▶ When can we speak of a "negotiation"?

- the parties are mutually dependent
- there is a conflict of interest
- an approximately equal balance of power exists
- agreement is considered the goal of the negotiation

▶ With what three factors can we measure the quality of a negotiation?

- effectiveness of the outcome (quality of the result)
- efficiency of the negotiating process (based on the time invested)
- the negotiating climate between the parties (quality of the relationship)

► **What are the criteria of a good negotiation result?**

A good negotiation result is:

- clear – without ambiguities
- feasible – no building castles in the air
- fair – no one is getting ripped off
- beneficial for both parties – based on the win-win principle
- sustainable – supported by both parties

2. GOOD PREPARATION IS HALF THE BATTLE

Poor preparation – the biggest negotiating mistake you can make

While preparing for negotiations, many negotiating teams neglect to discuss their different internal viewpoints, flesh out a unified strategy, and establish who will play what role in the negotiating process. If such discussions are then carried out during the actual negotiations, this ends up allowing the opposing party to learn useful information, such as who will be more likely to yield on certain points, who will be tougher to negotiate with, etc. This will usually give the opposing party a strategic advantage.

SELF-ASSESSMENT 2.1

Neil Reubens is at a job interview. He graduated two years ago with a degree in industrial engineering, then worked his way up to a junior managerial position at a company in Los Angeles. Now, seeking a new challenge, he has applied for a Project Manager position at an aerospace engineering company in Seattle, the city where his new girlfriend lives. The interview is going well – until the interviewer asks a crucial question.

INTERVIEWER: So, Mr. Reubens, what sort of salary are you expecting?

NEIL: How much do you usually offer professionals with two years of experience?

INTERVIEWER: You're just answering my question with another question – I'm interested in your own salary expectations.

NEIL: Well... I don't want to earn less than I'm currently earning.

INTERVIEWER: And how much are you currently earning, Mr. Reubens?

NEIL: At the moment, I'm taking home fifty thousand a year *(softly and without making eye contact)*. So obviously it should be a bit more now – I don't want to take a step down *(blushes and giggles sheepishly)*.

INTERVIEWER *(takes a deep breath and raises his eyebrows)*: Can you give more details about your current salary? How are the benefits? Do you get bonuses?

NEIL: Um, well, we don't get Christmas bonuses. And the benefits *(hesitates)*... But anyway, like I said, I want to get a bit more than I'm currently earning.

INTERVIEWER *(maintaining eye contact and silently waiting)*:...

NEIL: Well, I was hoping for ten percent more. Do you think that might be possible?

A week later, Neil gets the job offer. Unfortunately, his salary expectations have not been met. In any case, he is happy that the company is interested in hiring him. That evening, as he enjoys some wine with his girlfriend Nellie, the two of them wonder why Neil was not offered a higher salary.

WHAT EXACTLY DID NEIL DO WRONG IN HIS SALARY NEGOTIATION? LIST AT LEAST SIX THINGS!
Then read the solution at the end of the chapter.

Overestimating power

When we prepare for a negotiation, there is a tempting risk to overestimate our own power. We play out an idealized negotiation in our own fantasies and treat this imagined course of events as a probable outcome. This overestimation of one's own power can lead to presumptuous behavior – and is the most common type of mistake that can be observed in negotiations. What happens next? Having not accounted for the fact that everything could go entirely different than he has planned, the negotiator gets thrown completely off-track both strategically and emotionally. He has no alternative strategy when the situation demands one – and the other parties can take advantage of him when matters then escalate.

Underestimating power

Almost as common as overestimating power is the opposite – negotiators realizing in hindsight that they have *underestimated* their own position. Sellers think that the buyers hold all the power, while buyers think that the sellers hold all the power.

CASE STUDY: APARTMENT-HUNTING

Neil and Nellie have known each other for two months, and they have decided to move in together. They know they're taking it very quickly, but they're ready to give it a shot. They see a listing online for a charming apartment in the trendy Seattle neighborhood of Capitol Hill. "Man, we've got no chance of getting it," says Neil. "Hundreds of people must have called already – everybody wants a place like that. There's no use in even calling." "Nonsense," interjects Nellie. "None of those people are as nice as we are. We're dream tenants for any landlord – we're both employed, have no kids, earn good salaries... How many other people can say that?"

▶ QUESTION

In what ways are Neil and Nellie overestimating or underestimating their negotiating power?

▶ ANSWER

Neil presumes that everyone in the city wants to live in a modest apartment in a busy neighborhood, while Nellie presumes that there are not many other financially stable couples without kids in the city of Seattle. Both of their viewpoints have been shaped by their own personal perceptions and subjective interpretations of the situation.

How to realistically evaluate your position

The extent of your negotiating power depends largely upon the law of supply and demand. Even the most skilled negotiators are bound by the nature of the market. Thus, if you have something to offer which many people want and which is not widely available elsewhere, then you are in a very favorable position. And the reverse is also true – if what you are offering is widely available elsewhere yet not in great demand, then you do not have much bargaining power.

Negotiating has everything to do with markets and with the exchange of goods via markets. The word "market" itself comes from the Latin "mercatus" (trade, market) and "merx" (wares, merchandise, goods). A market is basically where supply and demand are brought together – for the exchange of goods as well as services and rights. Let's consider the used car market – a market with many buyers and sellers. Everyone has easy access to lots of information regarding used cars and market price ranges – they just need to go online, where any detail they may need is available on several major websites. Typical features of such a market are:

o The market is liquid – there are many buyers and sellers who are looking to do business with each other.
o The market is transparent – both buyers and sellers know who is offering which products at what prices.
o The market is homogeneous – all suppliers and consumers face the same conditions, with no functional differences.
o Individual buyers and sellers have no effect on market conditions, such as prices.

The more narrowly these conditions are met in a particular market, the more predictable the activities in that market will be. The negotiating power of a single individual generally is quite limited under these conditions. In other words, a single buyer or seller of a used car generally cannot influence the price very much, due to the liquidity, transparency, and homogeneity of the used car market. Such market conditions, however, are the exception.

Most markets are imperfect. They are not very liquid – with limited numbers of buyers and sellers, right up to the extreme case of monopolies. They are not fully transparent – with buyers and sellers generally not knowing who is buying or selling what items at what prices. And they are not homogeneous – with different parties facing different conditions, e.g., retail customers versus wholesale customers. It is these very market features that significantly affect the negotiating power of an individual party.

TIP:
The more imperfect a market is, the greater your chances of being able to use professional negotiation skills to exploit it.

In order to exploit the potential of imperfect markets, it is essential that you gather lots of information regarding the market in general, and regarding the opposing party in particular, while preparing for your actual negotiations. Make use of the following resources:

- Internet – search engine results, as well as the opposing party's own website
- Press archives – published market analyses
- Studies and reports – research results, relevant precedents, and official and unofficial expert opinions
- Personal experience – your own and others' personal experiences

Power is subjective

Bargaining power plays a decisive role in negotiations. There is a certain balance of power that exists in every negotiation – but the problem is that we seldom have all the information that we would need in order to accurately ascertain the true balance of power between parties. So we try to estimate it as best we can, using any means at our disposal, under the assumptions that...

- Power is what we believe it is.
- Power is what the other party believes it is.
- Power is what we believe the other party believes it is.

As such, many of the moves that we make during the negotiation process can be seen as attempts to influence either the opposing party's perceptions of our bargaining power or their perceptions of their own bargaining power – and there may be no better definition of "negotiating tactics" than this.

- Negotiating power means being able to say "no".
- Negotiating power means having a good alternative.
- Negotiating power means needing the deal less than the opposing party does.

Planning Tool 1: Questionnaire for effective preparation

Preparation is the first step of negotiation. This is when you jump right into things, looking forward and formulating the most realistic possible scenarios for your potential negotiations. The more effort you put into to your preparation, the more relaxed you will be when the time comes for the actual negotiations. You will be able to fully devote your efforts to analyzing and improving your baseline situation. Before any future negotiations, go through all of the questions in following checklist.

Questionnaire for effective preparation

1. **What higher goals are you pursuing?**
    - on a substantive level
    - on a personal level

2. **What is your concrete goal?**
    - What is the minimum that you hope to achieve?
    - What is your realistic goal?
    - What is your maximum goal?
    - What will be your opening offer?

3. **How is the balance of negotiating power between the parties?**

4. **How well do you know the opposing party?**
    - Do you have prior experience with them?
    - What can you find out about them?
    - What are their interests?
    - Do they have interests in common with your own?
    - What possible outcomes might benefit both sides?

5. **What information will you give the opposing party?**
   - What will you reveal?
   - What will you keep to yourself?

6. **What assumptions have you made?**

7. **Are you negotiating a single point or an entire "package"?**
   - What are the main points that comprise the package?
   - How are these interconnected?
   - Which points are particularly important to the opposing party?

8. **On which points are you willing to offer concessions?**

9. **What concessions can you demand from the opposing party?**

10. **Organizational**
    - Will you negotiate over the telephone, in writing, or in person?
    - Where will you meet (taking into account the "home-court advantage")?
    - Will you negotiate alone or with a team?
    - Who will play which roles on the team?
    - Are there time constraints?
    - By when must you achieve your desired result?

11. **How well are you prepared personally?**

    - How confident do you feel?
    - Where are you especially sensitive? ("hot buttons")
    - What will you do if the negotiation fails?
    - How much time are you willing to invest in this negotiation?

Planning Tool 2: S.M.A.R.T. goals

Nellie is sitting with her boss, Fleur, in the company cafeteria. They are going over an offer that they will soon present to a new client. Nellie will make the presentation, after which Fleur will handle the negotiations. Fleur is a 34-year-old Canadian who has been living in Seattle for only six months. She was previously based in Geneva and has gained lots of experience leading international teams in recent years.

From the very first contact with the client, Nellie notices how professionally Fleur approaches the negotiation. Nellie asks Fleur if she might be interested in mentoring her, and Fleur readily agrees. "So, what's the worst thing that an opposing party can do to you in a negotiation?" Nellie asks curiously. "Accepting my first offer," Fleur instantly replies. "Really? Why?" asks Nellie. "Think about it," says Fleur. "If they accept my first offer, then that means I could have gotten so much more. And I wouldn't be able to stop asking myself how much more would have been possible. It would mean that I wasn't ambitious enough." "Not ambitious enough?" asks Nellie.

"Yes, exactly. It's a matter of one's 'aspiration' – one's personal goal, the result that one is truly striving to achieve. In a sense, along with someone's bargaining power and their negotiation skills, this aspiration is the third major factor that drives the outcomes of their negotiations. The people who achieve the most – both in negotiations and in life – are the ones who set goals that are ambitious yet realistic. If someone sets their goals too high, then they'll never achieve them – but in reality, it's usually the opposite: people set their goals too *low*. Maybe they're not confident enough or maybe they lack self-esteem, I don't know what it is."

Fleur waits for Nellie to process this information. "So basically, people set their standards low so that they'll never be disappointed?" asks Nellie. "Exactly," replies Fleur. "There's a negotiation expert named Chester Karrass who spent many years working for Howard Hughes. He did lots of research into how negotiation works – and in one of his experiments, with 120 professional negotiators from the aerospace industry, he found that the negotiators who set realistically high expectations always got better results. They always came out ahead when matched up against parties who set their goals lower – even when those other parties had more bargaining power and better negotiation skills." "Wow," replies Nellie, amazed. "I'll be sure to set my goals accordingly from now on!" "Excellent – you can start with the S.M.A.R.T. model," suggests Fleur.

S.M.A.R.T. goal-setting criteria

S.M.A.R.T. is an acronym in which each letter stands for one of the five characteristics of well-formulated negotiation goals. Negotiators can evaluate their goals under these five criteria to ensure that their goals are clear, realistic, and ambitious. The more criteria a goal satisfies, the more definite that goal is. Get used to taking a second critical look, before each negotiation, at the goals you have formulated – and checking how you might be able to further adjust them.

S.M.A.R.T. goals are:

S = specific
M = measurable
A = attractive
R = realistic
T = time-bound

An example

"Nellie, you're planning on taking a vacation with Neil in February, right? And didn't you tell me that you wanted to go skiing while he wanted to go scuba diving? Now think about how you can go about setting your goal in a S.M.A.R.T. way," says Fleur, looking expectantly at Nellie. "Hmmm," Nellie thinks it over. "I'm going to propose that we go to Whistler (specific) during President's Day weekend (time-bound) – a friend of ours works there as a ski instructor and has offered to let us stay at his place. There's guaranteed snow (attractive). The ski pass costs $110, and we'll even get a 10% discount through our friend (measurable). And the whole plan is realistic – it's not like I'm asking to go heli-skiing in Norway!" "Sounds good," replies Fleur. "With regard to measurability, I'd suggest that you don't focus only on the price – but also, for example, on how quickly you can get there. I'll check back with you in March to see if you actually ended up going to Whistler!"

Planning Tool 3: BATNA – the best realistic alternative

During the course of any negotiation, you need to be clear about the fact that you always have alternatives outside the context of the negotiation. Thus, any negotiated result is a success if it is better than your best available alternative. The Harvard Method refers to this as the BATNA – the Best Alternative To a Negotiated Agreement. By having such an alternative, you avoid being dependent upon your counterpart in the negotiations. Any party that has no alternative to a negotiation, or only a very weak alternative, is always fundamentally at a disadvantage – and is automatically in a weaker negotiating position. It is thus essential that you know and understand both your own best realistic alternative *and* that of your counterpart.

Imagine that you are trying to sell an old record player at a flea market. Your hope to sell it for $50. After a short while, a prospective buyer offers you $30 – mentioning that he's seen a similar record player for $40 at another booth. Depending upon your negotiating skills, you would probably end up settling on a price somewhere between $35 and $45. However, as a professional negotiator, you have already thought about what you would do if no one were to show interest in the record player – you would gift it to your father for his birthday. He used to have a record player just like it and has told you how wonderful it was. In this alternative course of action, you would then save the $40 that you would have otherwise spent buying him basketball tickets as a birthday present. Knowing your BATNA, under no circumstances will you accept less than $40 for the record player.

How to develop your BATNA

- Create a list of your alternatives.
- Don't just stick with what comes to mind first.
- Think "outside the box". Be creative.
- Consider each alternative on your list:
  - Is it realistic?
  - Is it worth pursuing?
- Choose your BATNA.
- Then, also think about what your counterpart's BATNA would be.

How to make use of your BATNA

- If you have a good BATNA, then make sure your counterpart is well aware of the fact that you have such an alternative.
- If your BATNA is weak, then avoid letting your counterpart know this.
- If you think that your counterpart has a good BATNA, then avoid dwelling upon this – although your counterpart will probably keep bringing it up. Try to focus on selling the advantages of your own offer, so that their BATNA seems less attractive in comparison.
- If you suspect that your counterpart's BATNA is weak, then try to steer the conversation in that direction.
- Only agree to a negotiated solution if it is better than your BATNA.
- Do not threaten your counterpart with their own BATNA – rather, make clear to them the decision-making problem that they face.
- During the course of the negotiation, consider each party's second-best alternatives.

TIP:
A weak alternative will not help you in your negotiations – and will not give you any bargaining power. It is essential that you strengthen your BATNA before beginning your negotiation!

CASE STUDY: CARPOOLING

Neil has been working at the aerospace company for two weeks now. The offices are located 20 miles outside Seattle. Even though he is not earning any more money than he did before, he is getting an opportunity to gain valuable experience in a new area. Neil gets along well with his new colleagues – including Karim, the French employee with whom he shares an office, who also happens to be fairly new at the company. They soon discover that they live not far from each other. Karim offers to start picking Neil up each morning in his car, so that they can share gas costs. Neil likes the idea and quickly agrees.

That afternoon, as he takes the company's shuttle bus back to the city, from where he will catch a bus home, Neil wonders whether he has agreed too quickly to the carpooling idea. Karim had taken him by surprise, so Neil had not properly analyzed his alternatives and negotiated. In his spontaneity, Neil had completely forgotten to compare Karim's proposed solution against his own BATNA.

▶ QUESTION

What are Neil's potential BATNAs?

▶ ANSWER

- He can continue taking the company's shuttle bus – which is free – to the city and catching a bus from there.
- He can drive his own car, which is something that he enjoys doing and that would also give him the opportunity to study Spanish by listening to audiobooks on the way.
- As a triathlete, he can even cycle to work during the summer – which will help him keep fit for competitions.
- Since he is looking for a new apartment with his girlfriend and may move soon, he may have new commuting possibilities in the near future.

The next day, he goes over to Karim and explains why he has decided to cancel the carpooling arrangement to which he had hastily agreed. Karim, who had been looking forward to splitting the gas costs, is a bit disappointed.

Planning Tool 4: ZOPA – Zone of Possible Agreement

Negotiators generally have a sense of the zone in which they might be able to reach an agreement. This is known as the "ZOPA" – Zone of Possible Agreement. If you plan to sell your house, you will first think about how much you can realistically expect to receive for it – and based on whatever criteria you choose to evaluate, you will come up with some sort of acceptable price range.

An example

Suppose that Jonathan Miller has inherited a house near Miami from his grandmother. Jonathan lives in New York and has no intention of moving south, so he decides to sell the house. It's a small villa in excellent condition, built in the 1930s. It sits on a 13,000 sq. ft. plot in a quiet neighborhood; the average price for such a house in this particular suburb is around $800,000. The neighborhood is in very high demand at the moment, and there are not many houses up for sale there right now – so it's a great seller's market. At the same time, it's an unsecure global economic situation, so potential buyers are being a bit more hesitant about such large purchases. The bounds of Jonathan's ZOPA are determined by the following considerations:

- He wants to sell the house for at least $780,000.
- If he asks for more than $820,000, then potential buyers will likely be able to find more attractive offers on the market.
- Jan's ZOPA is thus the range between $780,000 and $820,000.

What are the benefits of knowing your ZOPA?

Setting such boundaries protects negotiators. If you are conscious of your ZOPA, then it becomes easier for you to resist any pressure or temptation, in the heat of the moment, to settle for less – no one will be able to coax you into making decisions that you would later regret.

If you negotiate in a team, then setting a ZOPA also prevents any individual team member from pressing ahead on their own and agreeing to something that has not been discussed beforehand with the other team members. And yet another benefit of setting a ZOPA is that it enables you to expressly limit the power of any agent or broker to whom you may delegate the actual negotiation process.

How to calculate your ZOPA

One reliable way to set the ZOPA is to utilize the BATNA concept. Your own BATNA thus defines the lower bound of the ZOPA – this is the least you would be willing to accept in the negotiations. And based on your presumptions as to what your counterpart's BATNA might be, you can determine their likely walk-away limit, which would represent the upper bound of the ZOPA – this is the maximum that you can possibly hope to achieve from the negotiations.

How large should your ZOPA be?

There is no precise answer here. Some ZOPAs are very narrow and precise, while others are broad and open-ended. One example of a narrow ZOPA would be the purchase of a mass-market product, such as shampoo. There are lots of companies that make shampoo, and the market is saturated – hundreds of thousands of shampoos are purchased each day by hundreds of thousands of consumers. It's a nearly perfect market. So the price of your shampoo will likely not be negotiable – or may be negotiable by a few cents at most. On the other hand, an example of a broad ZOPA would be if you were selling your classic sports car, a true collector's item. There aren't many like it around anymore, and neither you nor your potential buyers have any experience in selling or buying such cars. It's an imperfect market. There is a much greater scope for negotiation in this case – i.e., a broad zone of possible agreement.

Nibbling

Nellie and Fleur are going over their ideas one last time before their presentation to the client. "Nellie, I have one more tip for you: Don't forget about the nibbling!" says Fleur. "Nibbling? What do you mean?" asks Nellie, confused. "When I use the word 'nibbling'", explains Fleur, "I'm talking about how each side always knows that the other will not accept their initial offer, so you have to build in leeway for the other side to 'nibble' away at." "Oh, I understand," replies Nellie, "but that's how children behave – shouldn't we be able to forget about that kind of stuff in the context of professional negotiations?" "No," says Fleur, "remember that negotiation is all about two parties moving closer each other. The only question is how big each side's 'nibbles' will be. Last year, I was at a clothing market in China where the salesmen start off with prices that are 300% higher than what they can realistically expect a buyer to pay! Then there is a lively back-and-forth, played out according to unwritten rules that all the locals know, which eventually leads to predictable results.

That's obviously a special situation, unique to such markets – in general, though, the nibbling should be ambitious, yet not unreasonable." Nellie understands – and she's glad that their own negotiations won't follow the same rules as the Chinese markets. She discusses with Fleur how much 'nibble room' to build in to their initial offer in the upcoming negotiations.

Planning Tool 5: Information matrix

During the course of a negotiation, knowing how to handle information is extremely beneficial. To start, this involves gathering information in advance – since the more information you have, the more bargaining power you have. Imagine that, after not finding any decent rental options in two months of searching, Nellie and Neil decide to look into buying an apartment of their own. They check out a nice 3-bedroom apartment in a great location. Their information research reveals that a cell tower will soon be put up just down the street from the apartment. Nellie and Neil now have to consider whether they are still interested in purchasing it. At the very least, they have a strong argument for driving down the price.

So, one should gather as much information as possible when preparing for a negotiation – however, such information is only useful if one also knows how to analyze it.

For a structured analysis of the information that you have gathered during your preparation, make use of an information matrix. If, during the actual negotiations, new facts emerge in the lower two boxes (*keep* or *surprise*), then one should pause the negotiations in order to evaluate such information properly.

Information matrix

Give	Get
Information that we intend to give to the other party, either to enhance our bargaining power or to help pave the way towards an agreement. *For example: How far is the apartment from Nellie and Neil's workplaces? By when would they hope to move in? Does either of them plan to work from home? Do they expect to have children in the near future?*	Information that we want or need from the other party, either to enhance our bargaining power or to help pave the way towards an agreement. *For example: When will the current tenants be leaving? Does the building have a full-time caretaker? Are pets allowed? Is there central heating?*
Keep	**Surprise**
Information that we decide to keep to ourselves, so as not to reduce our own bargaining power. *For example: Neil and Nellie probably do not want to inform the potential seller that they have (somewhat prematurely) given notice to their landlord that they will be leaving their current apartment.*	Information that would surprise us if we were to learn of it during the course of the negotiation. *For example: If Nellie and Neil were to learn that the upstairs and downstairs neighbors have been locked in protracted legal battles with the landlord, then this information would come as a surprise.*

Checking assumptions

During the planning stage, we make all sorts of assumptions regarding the positions and goals of the other party – who will participate in the discussions, what the agenda will look like, how long the negotiations will last, how many competitors are involved, and so on. There is nothing wrong with making assumptions – if we don't go through things mentally beforehand, then we run the risk of being caught completely off guard when the moment comes. The important thing, however, is to always remind oneself that these are and remain only assumptions. So how can you check your assumptions? The easiest way is simply to ask. If you can identify your assumptions during the planning stage, then you can already prepare precise questions (for the "Get" box) through which your assumptions can be checked.

Assumptions regarding:	Ask:
■ Other interested parties ■ Opposing party's room for negotiation ■ Repairs that may need to be done ■ Recent renovations ■ Other properties the broker may have	■ Have you gotten a lot of interest in the apartment? ■ Is there a bit of flexibility in your asking price? ■ When was the last time the roof was redone? ■ The bathroom looks new; was it remodeled recently? ■ So, if we decide we're not interested in this apartment, do you have any similar ones available at the moment?

Planning Tool 6: Concession matrix

Negotiation is all about parties being flexible and moving towards each other. This process necessarily involves making concessions to the other party, showing our willingness to reach an agreement. If each side is rigidly sticking to its position, then negotiations will simply come to a standstill. This show of good will is the positive side of making concessions – the uncomfortable side is that we always have to give something up. We have to let go of some hope or expectation, and sometimes it hurts.

If we don't plan out our concessions, then we run the risk of either sticking to our position too rigidly or foolishly making big concessions too early. These risks are even greater when negotiating in a team.

The concessions that we will seek from the other party include, from a logical perspective, the range between the other party's opening offer and our minimum goal. From a psychological perspective, it also includes the range between their opening offer and our maximum goal – the only question then being the extent to which we can confidently negotiate towards this goal.

How to plan your concessions

You can make use of a "concession matrix" to plan out your concessions. Just like with the information matrix, it is advisable to take a short break before dealing with any concessions below the double line. These concessions either have personal consequences or bring new factors under consideration – so they should be thought over very carefully before you take action. If you are negotiating in a team, then you should also establish beforehand who will make any concessions. Your concessions should be prioritized accordingly:

- H - High priority: things that we absolutely must get/keep.
- M - Medium priority: things that we can give up without much distress.
- L – Low priority: things that are not so important, which we can readily give up.

Ideally, as a professional negotiator, you would like to exchange concessions that have lower priority for you for concessions that have higher priority for the opposing party.

Give	Get
Concessions that we plan to make to the other party – things that we will readily give up in order to come to an agreement. *For example: In his salary negotiations, Neil might plan to offer to give up some benefits in exchange for a more flexible work schedule.*	Concessions that we will demand from the other party when we make a concession of our own. Or concessions that we request when we are in a stronger position, in order to signal that we are looking to move towards an agreement. *For example: Neil intends to pursue an MBA degree; he would like the company to contribute towards his professional education costs.*

Keep	Surprise
Concessions that we absolutely do not want to make – that would take us below the lower bound of our ZOPA. *For example: Under no circumstances will Neil accept a lower salary than he earned at his previous job.*	Concessions that would surprise us if the opposing party were to make or demand them during the course of the negotiations. *For example: If Neil were to find out, during the course of the negotiation, that the job would require him to supervise projects on the ground in Russia and Afghanistan, then he would need to ask for some time to think over the consequences of this new employment condition.*

Planning Tool 7: Planning complex negotiations

When we negotiate only one issue, such as a purchase price, it is relatively easy to identify our goals, bargaining room, interests, BATNAs, ZOPA, and concessions. But for complex negotiations, it gets more confusing. In complex negotiations:

- There is more than one thing being negotiated.
- These things are linked and are more or less dependent upon each other.
- This interdependency can be logical (buying a house also involves buying a plot of land) or tactical (booking early can yield a discount).
- The order/value of the things is difficult to define.

The "one-way street" agenda

Most negotiators plan out their negotiations as a one-way street – in other words, they go through the individual topics of negotiation one by one, in order. This sequential approach has the advantage of a logical structure, making it easy for less experienced negotiators. But such an approach is risky – if the negotiations reach an impasse, then the next items on the agenda will often suffer from a tense atmosphere in which the parties are less willing to negotiate.

The "roundabout" agenda

The much more flexible approach is the "roundabout" model – which is especially well-suited for complex negotiations with numerous points to be negotiated. Under this approach, the individual points of negotiation are each dealt with on a provisional basis, with none of them being finalized until the completed deal is finalized. This enables the parties to develop complex solutions to complex issues, giving proper consideration to the interdependent nature of the various points being discussed. The possibility of bringing already-discussed topics back into play enables them to explore new, creative combinations as they work towards an agreement. Visually, this approach can be represented as a roundabout, or traffic circle, in which the parties can freely "drive" the discussions back and forth between any of the individual points of access at any time. In general, it is much easier to reach a compromise by considering various issues together, rather than by addressing and finalizing one individual point after another. Using the roundabout approach, negotiating parties never lose sight of the big picture.

The "negotiation nexus"

A "negotiation nexus" can help you prepare to negotiate using the roundabout approach.

- Instead of a list of negotiation topics, there is a diagram – a sort of "mind map".
- It shows the main points to be negotiated (rarely more than four or five)
- It shows how these points of discussion are interconnected.
- It defines limits, goals, and opening positions.
- It shows the systematic maneuverability between the different points.

In the negotiation nexus that Neil and Nellie have created for their apartment purchase, it is easy to understand how the individual points of negotiation mutually affect each other. Neil and Nellie can immediately see that if they want to replace the skylight, then they have less funds available for the down payment, which in turn would mean taking out a bigger loan. The negotiation nexus enables them to keep sight of the big picture, play around with the various parameters, and explore different scenarios. It is essential to have your negotiation nexus written down – it is much easier to explore your possible courses of action if you can visualize them in front of you. Neil and Nellie can use their negotiation nexus both amongst themselves and in their negotiations with the bank.

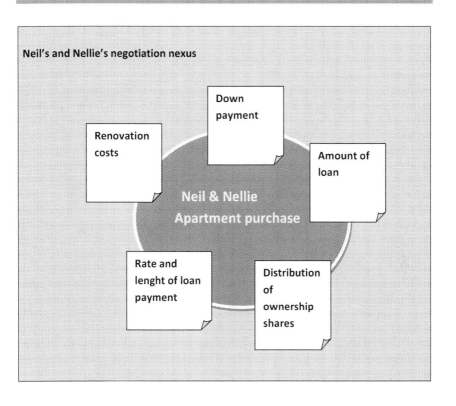

Neil's and Nellie's negotiation nexus

Down payment

Renovation costs

Amount of loan

Neil & Nellie
Apartment purchase

Rate and lenght of loan payment

Distribution of ownership shares

"Funny money"

Nellie and Fleur meet up over lunch in the company cafeteria, and Nellie proudly updates Fleur on her planning for the apartment purchase. "We've worked through our negotiation nexus really well – our path forward is clear now," she says. "Congratulations!" replies Fleur. "Are you prepared for 'funny money' tactics?" "'Funny money' tactics? What do you mean?" asks Nellie – it's yet another term with which she is not familiar. "Well," explains Fleur, "'funny money' covers everything of value that is not expressly included in the price of the thing being negotiated. For example, in the case of your apartment purchase, there may be closing costs, interest, real estate transfer tax, brokerage fees, lawyer fees, moving costs, installation of a new kitchen, etc. And you know what? 'Funny money' is usually not really funny at all – because it misleads people. We end up getting ourselves into things that cost much more than they seem. Do you know why kitchen manufacturers offer free installation of their products? Do you think the company is just offering you this service for free because they like you? They've probably hidden the installation costs somewhere else. So always stay alert and watch out for funny money!" Nellie sighs, knowing that she will have to go over her plan with Neil yet again.

Planning Tool 8: Core concerns – preparing yourself emotionally

Proper negotiation preparation using Planning Tools 1-7 is immensely beneficial – you will have much more success in your future negotiations with the help of these tools. If you want to boost your success even more, make sure that you are also emotionally prepared for your negotiations. How can you prepare yourself emotionally for negotiations?

First, you need to understand that human beings do not negotiate in a purely rational manner – our emotions always play a role as well. Many of you are probably familiar with psychologist Paul Watzlawick's "iceberg" model of communication. Only a small portion of a typical iceberg can be seen above the surface of the water – the majority of the iceberg remains hidden below the surface. It's the same with communication. Only a small portion of all communication is "visible"

– what we can see, hear, read, or otherwise learn from statements, written offers, agreements, research, facts, and figures. But the much greater, invisible portion of communication concerns things such as needs and motivations, which are closely bound with emotions. During the course of a negotiation, we experience joy and anger, surprise and annoyance, satisfaction and frustration. There is no such thing as an emotionless negotiation. And when two icebergs meet, they collide below the surface.

When negotiations get stuck or collapse, it is partly due to irreconcilable differences on a substantive level – but most often, there are problems in the relationship between the parties that are ultimately responsible for the deadlock. Both sides, with their respective emotions, contribute to this. We must thus prepare ourselves for this aspect of negotiation as well, learning to keep our coolness in difficult situations and not simply react emotionally.

The five core concerns

In their 2005 book *Beyond Reason*, which builds upon the classic *Getting to Yes*, Harvard researchers Roger Fisher and Daniel Shapiro discuss extensively the role that emotions play in negotiations. The main point of the book is that there are five "core concerns" that drive our behavior – and when these core concerns are threatened, it automatically generates negative emotions that cause us react without thinking rationally. In other words, we no longer react in a conscious manner. We say and do things which we cannot take back and which we will later regret. Fisher and Shapiro thus recommend that we deal with our own hot buttons before the negotiations – and also consider where the other side is most sensitive and might need to be handled with kid gloves.

The five core concerns are:

- appreciation
- affiliation
- autonomy
- status
- role

Appreciation

Everyone wants their actions to be recognized and appreciated. Imagine the following situation: You are working on a team. You usually end up keeping the minutes of the team meetings – you figure somebody's got to do it, and it's generally no trouble at all for you. But the other team members soon start taking for granted that you're going to keep the minutes at every meeting. In one meeting, after your workload has increased due to another project you are handling, you suggest that someone else record the minutes. The response? "Oh, just handle it yourself – you've got so much experience with it by now." And then they move right on to the first agenda item. How would you feel in such a situation? Probably frustrated, feeling like your involvement was not being appreciated. Maybe the minutes of this meeting will end up being sparser, or maybe you will be less likely to volunteer for such tasks in the future. The desire for recognition is one of our basic needs. When it is infringed upon, we react with negative emotions.

Affiliation

Just like we want to be appreciated, we also want to feel like we belong to someone. We want to be affiliated – to be a part of something. Being excluded hurts. We want to be kept in the loop when there is information we should know; we don't want to be marginalized within our group. Imagine you're working on a negotiation team. It always seems like your colleague has been fully informed by your supervisor – while you always seem to be lacking important pieces of information. "Get in touch with Mr. X if you've got any questions," your boss tells customers, pointing at your colleague with a smile. "He's up-to-date on everything." How would you feel in this case? What emotions would you carry into future interactions with your boss and your colleague? And how would your future negotiations with this client play out? You would probably be dispirited, irritated, or even angry, depending upon how you personally deal with such situations. In any case, the infringement of your basic need for affiliation would certainly have repercussions in the negotiations.

Autonomy

The need for autonomy is our third core concern. As human beings, we want to be able to make our own decisions. We feel like our independence is being constrained when someone else makes decisions behind our back without involving us – or, even worse, tells us what to do. Imagine the following situation: As a purchaser for a large company, you are in charge of buying the company's computer systems. While meeting with an important supplier to negotiate the price of their machines, he barks at you, "You have to pay for the changes to the specs – it's your own fault that we had to keep changing things. Get your boss to the table now so we can discuss this." You would probably think (and maybe even reply), "Who are you to tell me to do?" In any case, further discussions would probably not proceed in a relaxed, constructive manner.

Status

The fourth core concern is for the recognition of one's status. Our societies are organized in a hierarchical manner. Even in small families, for example, we differentiate between parents and children; in larger families, between the head of the family and the rest of the clan. In companies, asymmetrical relationships include those between managers and employees, as well as between suppliers and customers. There are unwritten rules and behavioral norms that reflect the nature of these relationships. Those with lower status defer to those with higher status – and in most cases, it is those with higher status who take the lead in negotiation decision-making. People feel offended when their status is not recognized. It is rare for a low-level employee to tell a high-level manager, "You know, the presentation is not really convincing – I think you need to work on it a bit more." This basic need for the recognition of one's status varies in strength between different cultures. It is especially strong in Asian, Arab, and Latin American cultures, while it is of lesser importance in societies like Scandinavia or the Netherlands. Corporate culture also plays a role in this. In a particularly hierarchical company, people are more focused on their status, which can even determine something as basic as who gets which parking space. On the other hand, in companies with flatter hierarchies, the need to have one's status recognized is less pronounced.

Role

The fifth core concern is our need for recognition of the different roles that we carry out. Imagine that you're called into your boss' office – an important client is very angry about something. Someone will need to stay at work late today to resolve the problem, and the only question is who. You know that this client is very difficult, always making special requests that end up requiring lots of extra work – and this particular work would probably keep you at the office until midnight. Tonight also happens to be a particularly bad night for you – it's your anniversary, and your wife has bought theater tickets. Three different roles collide in this example. You would like to be a dutiful employee, a client-oriented professional, and a considerate spouse – all at once. You thus face an inner conflict with contradictory emotions – and this does not facilitate your negotiation at all. Emotions that arise out of conflicting roles are often hidden, which means that it is difficult to understand the behavior of negotiating parties without knowing the underlying causes for such behavior. Unfortunately, we rarely get to know about our counterparts' "hidden agendas".

How to prepare yourself with regard to the five core concerns

CASE STUDY: JUST WHAT I NEEDED TODAY!

Fleur is planning to have a talk with Nellie. She is quite angry. Nellie's performance has not been very good over the last few weeks, and Fleur doesn't want to hear any excuses. She knows that Nellie and Neil are in the middle of a stressful apartment search, but she wants Nellie to pull herself together anyway going forward – to start making her deadlines, showing up for meetings on time, and paying more attention to spelling and grammar in her presentations. She also wants Nellie to show more commitment to her job and finally make some progress on her three outstanding projects. As if the situation with Nellie wasn't bad enough, Fleur is dealing with a terrible migraine. "Oh, great, just what I needed today!" thinks Fleur.

▶ QUESTION

What can Fleur do to prepare herself emotionally for her conversation with Nellie?

▶ ANSWER

Fleur makes a cup of tea, gets out her iPhone, finds her favorite Jack Johnson song, closes her office door, and stands on her head for five minutes. She then puts her feet up on her desk, grabs a notepad and a pen, takes a deep breath – and starts scratching out some notes.

▶ ANALYSIS

Appreciation:
Fleur would really like to vent her frustrations – however, as a seasoned negotiator, she does not do so, knowing that it is important to avoid blaming or accusing Nellie. If Fleur were to allow herself to get carried away because of her migraine, she could end up making Nellie feel like she did not appreciate any of the good work that Nellie has done.

Affiliation:
Fleur decides to be more transparent with Nellie regarding the short- and long-term goals and strategies of both the department and the company – this way, Nellie will better understand why it is so important that she complete her three outstanding projects. Moreover, Nellie will identify more strongly with the company, and

this stronger sense of affiliation will likely make her take her responsibilities more seriously.

Autonomy:
Ideally, Fleur would like to create a step-by-step plan for Nellie, spelling out in detail everything Nellie had to do, which Nellie would then have to work through, sign, and submit to Fleur after completion. Fleur will not do so, however – because then Nellie would feel as if she were being treated like a baby. As an independent, responsible employee, Nellie wants to be actively involved in finding solutions, not simply ordered around like a child.

Status:
Fleur knows that Nellie has started to see her more as a friend, rather than as a boss. She plans to again make clear to Nellie that, as Nellie's manager, she is responsible for the results of the entire team – and must also make sure that other employees don't get stuck with more work because of Nellie's slacking off. Nellie has no special status in the company.

Role:
Fleur would love to continue mentoring Nellie, supporting Nellie's professional development, and sharing all her knowledge and experience. However, Fleur knows that, when looking at her different roles, her responsibilities as a manager clearly take priority.

In order to prepare for her conversation with Nellie in the example from the case study, Fleur jotted down notes to help her become more conscious of her core concerns. You can use the following checklist to think through your own core concerns. Note down any key points that will help ensure that you and your negotiating partners stay steady emotionally, thus greatly helping you avoid escalation of any problems that may arise in the course of the negotiations.

"Core concerns" checklist

Core concern	My core concerns	What will I express openly in this regard?	Possible core concerns of the other party	What can I say or do to bolster the other party emotionally?
Appreciation				
Affiliation				
Autonomy				
Status				
Role				

SOLUTION TO SELF-ASSESSMENT 2.1

1. Neil has not thought about his salary expectations beforehand. He is not even clear about the benefits he is getting at his current job.

2. Due to his lack of experience with salary negotiations, Neil is unable to improvise confidently – prior to the interview, he should have researched how to handle such discussions.

3. Neil has not set minimum/maximum salary goals to define the framework within which his salary negotiations should take place.

4. Neil's insecure demeanor (hesitation, giggling, lack of eye contact) leaves a weak impression as well.

5. It is clear that Neil is uncomfortable discussing salary, and he reacts nervously to the interviewer's continued questioning on the topic. He loses focus and starts repeating himself.

6. Neil has not prepared any arguments about the value he would bring to the company thanks to his qualifications and experience – he offers absolutely nothing to convince the interviewer that he deserves a higher salary. He does not seem to know the market value of his own work.

SUMMARY: GOOD PREPARATION IS HALF THE BATTLE

▶ **How to prepare for negotiations**

- Start by realistically taking stock of your bargaining power. Remember to be honest about your potential weaknesses.
- Work continuously to increase your bargaining power.
- Thoroughly think through your "core concerns" (your true needs, goals, and motivations) as well as your personal limitations.
- Also think about the other side's core concerns – and about what preventive actions you can take in this regard.

- If you will be negotiating in a team, it is essential that agreement be reached beforehand regarding the strategy that the team will pursue.
- Be open to new ideas that can contribute to finding solutions. Plan to involve the other party.
- Prepare yourself with written notes (of both your research and your own thoughts). Use the points below to guide you.

▶ Your minimum

The minimum that you can accept in a negotiation is your BATNA – and anything that you can achieve in the negotiation to improve upon your best alternative should be considered a success. **Note:** Anything less than this should not even be considered – you can always fall back on your BATNA.

▶ Your goal

Your goal should be ambitious but realistic – near the upper bound of your ZOPA. The more ambiguous your ZOPA is, the more leeway you have to set bold goals. **Note:** A goal is not simply a wish – it is a result that you will actually *commit* yourself to work towards.

▶ Your opening position

In your opening offer, you need to leave room beyond your goal for the other party to "nibble" away. Again, the goal itself should be realistic. **Note:** Negotiations almost always involve a "package", with several points to be negotiated.

▶ An extreme opening position...

- always undermines one's credibility, and
- usually leads to a stalemate or
- making very large concessions, which entails risk.

3. UNDERSTANDING NEGOTIATION AS A PROCESS

The three levels of negotiation

Negotiation is a complex affair – we are constantly working on several levels at the same time. It can be compared to cooking: a good chef knows his guests, knows his ingredients, has a few tricks up his sleeve, and knows how to salvage an oversalted dish. And one who is still learning how to cook simply needs recipes to guide him, step-by-step, through the process of adding ingredients; he can then successfully prepare an entire meal – i.e., achieve his goal result.

In negotiations, we operate on three levels:

- o content – the substantive level (the actual product/service being negotiated, with related knowledge, facts, figures, and agreements)
- o continue – the methodological level (how the negotiation is carried out, including the techniques/structure employed by the parties)
- o contact – the psychological level (your own emotions, as well as the emotions of your counterparts)

Highly experienced negotiators can confidently navigate between these different levels – just like a master chef at a four-star restaurant can create culinary delights without much preparation beforehand, deftly combining ingredients on the basis of his experience alone. On the other hand, a young chef might still rely on cookbooks and checklists to help him prepare the perfect meal – likewise, young negotiators find it helpful to follow guidelines. Even master chefs and seasoned negotiators, however, never stop learning – they constantly work on perfecting their craft.

The negotiation process

When negotiating, one should not skip any steps of the process. The word "N.E.G.O.T.I.A.T.E." itself provides a useful mnemonic, with each letter representing one stage of the negotiation process.

1. Names and niceties
2. Establish general conditions
3. Get standpoints exchanged
4. Observe and identify common ground
5. Take note of differences
6. Initiate negotiation
7. Agreement
8. Task distribution
9. End – celebrate and say farewell

Names and niceties

The first step of a negotiation is the personal introduction of the parties to each other, if necessary. Some small talk follows, as the two parties establish a relationship. In cultures where the communication style is more direct – including many western countries – these formalities generally amount to just a few words or a few minutes at most. In cultures with a more indirect communication style – including many Asian, Arab, and eastern European countries – the relationship-building process can take considerably longer and is invariably highly important to the success of all future interactions between the parties. In such cultures, this process can last anywhere from a few hours (in the form of a drawn-out business lunch, for example, as is common even in a country like France) to several days (as is the custom in several Arab countries). It is important to be patient when negotiating in a culture that communicates more indirectly; wait for your counterparts to signal that it is time to get down to business. On the other hand, when negotiating in a culture that communicates more directly, do not be surprised if your counterparts start discussing the issues right away. They likely see small talk as superfluous – and there is usually more than enough time for it later.

Establish general conditions

Together with your counterparts, set the framework and ground rules for the discussion before starting to negotiate the substantive issues. How much time do you have to reach an agreement? What are the parties' expectations? What are the goals for today – a signed contract? an agreement in principle? or just a preliminary exchange of ideas regarding the way forward? Is there a provisional agenda that sets out the points to be discussed? Do you need someone to moderate the discussions? Who will keep the minutes of the meetings? Are there any other ground rules that need to be set (e.g., switching off cell phones)? You can also clarify at this point who is authorized to take decisions for the two sides – are the meeting participants authorized to take binding decisions on behalf of their companies, or will they need to get approval from their higher-ups?

Get standpoints exchanged

Now it's time to get down to business. At this stage, the two parties will exchange information regarding where they stand and what they are seeking. The negotiation process is most effective when each side knows and understands clearly what the other side wants. Each side should have two things prepared: their *opening statement* and their *opening position*.

Your opening statement should describe your needs, wishes, interests, and expectations with regard to the current negotiations, as well as with regard to the long-term relationship with the other party. Why are you here? What are you seeking to accomplish in the short and long term? What is your ultimate goal? This exchange will result in a discussion in which each side tries to understand what the other hopes to achieve. This stage of the negotiation process is marked by acute questioning and active listening on the part of both parties.

Of course, we also want to share our opening position and find out the other party's opening position – clear, unambiguous statements of what each side is asking for. If either of the parties refuses to share their opening position, then it will be very difficult for negotiations to proceed.

Observe and identify common ground

When the opening positions have been exchanged, it quickly becomes clear just how far apart the two parties are. At this point, we are often tempted to immediately think about what we can get from the other side – what concessions we can get them to make right away. But this is usually a mistake; it can quickly lead the negotiations into a dead end. It is often more effective to first outline the common ground that the two parties share with regard to their interests, etc. This will be helpful later on, when we try to identify new, mutually beneficial solutions together. Giving negotiating parties the sense that they have something in common also helps get the negotiations off on a positive note. Moreover, it subconsciously makes the two parties more willing to make concessions when the time comes.

Take note of differences

At this point, there is obviously a gap between the parties! And if we have properly prepared, we know our minimum goal, our most realistic goal, and the maximum goal that we are committed to pursuing. At this stage, it's all about the two parties assuming the differences between them in a manner that allows the atmosphere to remain relaxed – recognizing each other's demands, without accepting them. Have the other party confirm your understanding of what they are seeking – and check whether they have correctly understood your own position as well.

Initiate negotiation

Now is the time to actually negotiate – and close the gap between the parties. You have a choice of strategies here. You can negotiate competitively with a focus on your own performance, or you can pursue the most fair, equitable solution for both parties. You can also trade concessions or develop creative solutions that benefit both sides – which is obviously the most effective path.

Agreement

Once you believe that the gap between the parties has been closed and an agreement has been reached, you should outline your understanding of this agreement and check whether the other party is of the same understanding – if so, the deal can be closed. There are some negotiators who will try to knock extra concessions out of you at this stage of the process – depending upon the balance of power, as well as your own BATNA, you can consider whether you are willing to grant such concessions.

Task distribution

What are the next steps? Who will take care of them? By when? Do we need a written contract? When will it be signed? Do we need to get official approval from the company for our proposed agreement? Do we need some more time to clear up loose ends? Draw up a concise outline of action items.

End – celebrate and say farewell

Close the negotiations in a clear-cut fashion. Decide how you will celebrate your success and part ways. In some cultures, the signing of a formal document alone does not necessarily signify that the parties are truly in accord – so if a serious commitment based on mutual trust is important to you, then it often pays to invest more effort into relationship-building. This can include things like dinners (with or without alcohol) or cultural events (from the opera to sporting events to karaoke). Don't forget: When one negotiation finishes, it's only a matter of time until the next one begins.

SELF-ASSESSMENT 3.1

▶ TASK

Read through the statements below and quickly decide which ones are incorrect.

Names and niceties
a. I'm glad you could make it. How was your trip?
b. Let me introduce you to our team.
c. So, here's what we need...

Establish general conditions
a. This is what's on the agenda for today...
b. Let's see if we can get this agreement done today!
c. We can take a ten-minute break every two hours – does that sound good?

Get standpoints exchanged
a. Long-term cooperation is very important to us.
b. We're interested in a product that meets our high quality standards.
c. We can offer you $580,000 for the house – that's our final offer.

Observe and identify common ground
a. We're really not very familiar with your culture there in China.
b. So, both of us are looking for a solution that our companies will go along with.
c. You've really offered us excellent service over the last five years.

Take note of differences
a. I'm afraid the price you've quoted is a bit higher than what we were expecting.
b. What exactly are your issues with our offer?
c. We're still not really sure about what kind of terms we can provide you.

Initiate negotiation
a. So if we give you the 10% discount, then what would we get in return?
b. We need the delivery right away – otherwise there's no deal.
c. Whatever you need, we can give you.

Agreement
a. Let me just summarize the main points we've discussed here today.
b. I'm not really sure this is what we want, but...
c. Let's take one more look at what we've agreed upon.

Task distribution
a. So then... till next time!
b. When can you send me a draft of the contract?
c. Let's make a list of the next steps we need to take.

End – celebrate and say farewell
a. Thanks for all the time and effort you've invested!
b. Are you interested in going to the football game with us this Sunday?
c. I was afraid we'd never actually come to an agreement!

The solution to self-assessment 3.1 can be found at the end of the chapter.

The "helicopter view"

You are now familiar with the three levels of negotiation and you know how important it is to follow all of the steps in the negotiation process – N.E.G.O.T.I.A.T.E. So you now have all the tools that you need to pause at any time during your negotiations and check:

- Where do we stand right now?
- Are we on the right path?
- Are things going as planned?
- Do I need to reorient myself?
- Do I need to get the entire process back on track?

Take a "helicopter view" of your negotiations. A helicopter always hovers above the action, dissociated from it. Psychologists define "dissociation" as a state in which you experience events or situations as if "from the outside". If you can successfully take a critical look at your negotiations in a dissociated manner at any point during the process, then this will be of great benefit for you.

CASE STUDY: HOUNDED

It's Saturday morning. Nellie has spent the night at her boyfriend Neil's place – along with her dog Rowdy. Nellie and Neil had gone out dancing and had only returned home in the wee hours. At 7 o'clock, the phone starts ringing off the hook. Nellie drowsily answers. An angry neighbor, Mr. Rossi, starts snapping at her across the line. "I couldn't sleep a wink all night – your mutt didn't stop barking for a second! I've had enough of this! This building doesn't even allow pets. Keep it at your own house next time!" Nellie manages to calm him down and put off the discussion until noon, when she will be awake enough to settle the matter amicably with him.

▶ TASK

How should Nellie and Neil proceed to carry out the negotiation with Mr. Rossi in a structured manner? Play out the situation with a partner, or jot down your own notes.

▶ ANALYSIS

Here's how the discussion might go:

N. Nellie and Neil might welcome Mr. Rossi to their apartment with a cappuccino – they know he loves coffee. They might then apologize for Rowdy's barking and the fact that it might have kept the neighbors awake.

E. They can then suggest figuring out a solution to the problem together.

G. If Mr. Rossi agrees, the two sides can take turns presenting their points of view on the matter. Nellie might explain how she has no one else to look after Rowdy, while Mr. Rossi might talk about how the lack of sleep will affect his work at the pizzeria.

O. Neil can point to the fact that he and Mr. Rossi have always gotten along well, particularly when they brought certain issues to the landlord together.

T. Mr. Rossi might want to specifically point out here that Rowdy would not be allowed to live in the apartment.

I. The two sides can now think about possible solutions together: "What if..."

A. They might agree that Nellie will find a dog-sitter, or that Neil and Mr. Rossi will have a talk with the landlord about the lack of soundproofing in the building.

T. Nellie might suggest that the two sides have a quick talk again next month to check whether the situation has improved.

E. Mr. Rossi might invite Nellie and Neil to his pizzeria for some delicious homemade pasta and Italian wine.

SOLUTION TO SELF-ASSESSMENT 3.1

Names and niceties
c. So, here's what we need...
-> neglecting small talk, trying to get to the point too quickly

Establish general conditions
b. Let's see if we can get this agreement done today!
-> too vague, doesn't clearly define any structure for the negotiations to follow

Get standpoints exchanged
c. We can offer you $580,000 for the house – that's our final offer.
-> stating a final position, ruling out any negotiating room

Observe and identify common ground
a. We're really not very familiar with your culture there in China.

-> stressing differences rather than commonalities

Take note of differences
c. We're still not really sure about what kind of terms we can provide you.
-> when one side expresses itself so vaguely, it remains unclear how much of a gap actually exists between the parties

Initiate negotiation
b. We need the delivery right away – otherwise there's no deal.
-> too hard-line – sounds like a threat
c. Whatever you need, we can give you.
-> too soft – will probably be taken advantage of

Agreement
b. I'm not really sure this is what we want, but...
-> the solution is probably not sustainable, so it would be better to ask what is missing in order to reach a satisfactory result

Task distribution
a. So then... till next time!
-> (neglects to set out concretely the next steps to be taken)

End – celebrate and say farewell
c. I was afraid we'd never actually come to an agreement!
-> doesn't really make the other party look forward to the next negotiation

SUMMARY: UNDERSTANDING NEGOTIATION AS A PROCESS

- Familiarize yourself with the N.E.G.O.T.I.A.T.E. process – it represents the fundamental structure for any negotiation.
- Take a "helicopter view" of your negotiation to check where you stand in the process.
- Make sure that your behavior conforms to the current step of the process.
- Only move on to the next step once the objective of the current step has been achieved.

4. BASIC NEGOTIATION TACTICS

Proceeding tactically: How-to

We all quickly learn that being tactical gives us an advantage when we negotiate. In this chapter, we will discuss some fundamental rules of thumb and familiarize you with essential negotiation tactics. We will also take a closer look at the special case of coalition-building.

The goal of this chapter is to provide you with tactical know-how that will be an indispensable element of your actual negotiation. Although different, *tactics* and *strategies* are closely intertwined. While both require the proper application of certain tools, a strategy is generally geared towards achieving an overarching goal, whereas a tactic is a short-term measure towards achieving a short-term, interim goal. Your strategy is your big-picture plan – your basic course of action. Often framed in the medium or long term, it might define your overall vision or mission. Your strategy in a negotiation typically includes the question of how you will act towards the other side generally – e.g., whether you will take a cooperative stance or a competitive stance. A tactic, on the other hand, is defined by Merriam-Webster as "an action or method that is planned and used to achieve a particular goal." In other words, tactics are the procedures that you employ, within the means at your disposal, to achieve your short-to medium-term objectives.

SELF-ASSESSMENT 4.1

Neil has been called into his boss' office. He has no idea why.

DR. SCHUSTER: Mr. Reubens, you've been working with us for two months now – are you happy here?

NEIL: Yes, very happy. I've settled into the work quite well, and I like my coworkers too.

DR. SCHUSTER: Glad to hear it. Then you're up for a special challenge, right?

NEIL: Sure. What's it all about?

DR. SCHUSTER: I need you to handle a project for us in Germany. We're getting ready for the ILA Air Show in Berlin, and I think you're just the right person for it. Starting next Monday, you'll spend 8 weeks prepping on-site. The exhibition itself will last 4 days. I know it's short notice, but I'm sure you can handle the job! And you'll get a nice taste of Berlin too.

NEIL: But I'm already wrapped up in another project – will I get someone else to help me on it?

DR. SCHUSTER: Well, you know we're very short-staffed right now. But this is your chance to prove yourself – I know you can do it!

Dr. Schuster stands up and walks Neil to the door.

▶ WHAT TACTICS HAS DR. SCHUSTER EMPLOYED?

Try to identify at least three things that made it difficult for Neil to get a leg up in the discussion.

As always, you can find the solution at the end of the chapter.

The importance of getting off to a good start

As mentioned in the previous chapter, two items necessary for getting a negotiation started in a professional manner are the *opening statement* and the *opening position*. Both of these elements serve all three levels of a negotiation. We want to work with competent dialogue partners (*substantive level*), we want to know the goal of the negotiations, the opposing party's demands, and the planned procedure of the negotiations (*methodological level*), and we want to understand with whom we are negotiating (*psychological level*).

Opening the negotiation – your "overture"

The start of a negotiation can be compared to an opera's overture. This instrumental introductory piece, often played before the curtain even rises, typically sets forth the main musical themes of the work. In the same way, the "overture" of a negotiation sets the tone for the rest of the discussions that will occur between the parties.

The overture plays a harmonizing role, as the two parties find out more about each other. In this opening phase, one often hears statements about the parties themselves, their products and services, joint successes in the past, future opportunities – and naturally the items on the day's agenda. There is sometimes a covert power struggle going on behind these statements. Some of the key questions at this stage are:

- Who will take the lead in the negotiations? Formally or informally?
- Who is in control? Do the parties have equal bargaining power?
- How can I put my strategy into action?
- Can I already pick up on the other party's strategy?

TIP:
During the opening phase of the negotiations, it is not yet about what the parties want; rather, it is about getting ready and setting the tone for the discussions. The agenda itself plays an interesting role here – take the time to work with the other party to fine-tune it.

The role of the agenda

Your agenda will contain the points to be discussed with the other party as you negotiate towards an agreement. The setting of the agenda itself is your first opportunity to work on something together with your counterpart – and if you are strategically aiming for a win-win solution, then you should take advantage of this opportunity! An agenda that is adopted jointly with the other party is a clear signal of cooperation, whereas a unilaterally presented agenda is often the first serious sign that you are headed towards a win-lose result. An open, transparent outline of discussion points also fosters cooperation – whereas not disclosing an agenda is likely to have the opposite effect. What you do need to think about is whether you will set out only a broad framework or a more detailed plan for the discussion. This decision will be based upon whatever preferences you and your counterpart may have, with respect to your individual communication styles.

Your opening position

The first clear, unambiguous statement of what you want is contained in your opening position. Exchange opening positions with your counterpart only after the "overture". If necessary, pause the discussion to revise the proposal that you have prepared. Do not make any concessions until after you find out the other party's opening position.

Your opening position must be substantively credible and must be communicated authentically. You want to give the impression that it is close to what the final agreement should look like. Ideally, you would like the other party to state their opening position first. However, convention dictates that, when buying and selling, it is usually the seller who states their price first.

TIP:
Sometimes the other party's opening position may bring up new information regarding what they are seeking, and you may find yourself needing to quickly revise your own opening position. If necessary, ask for a brief pause to think things through!

How to reach a result – many roads lead to Rome

There are as many ways to reach a goal as there are people in the world. While diplomats seek harmonized and counterbalanced resolutions, the bazaars and markets of the world are full of spirited haggling with lots of emotions at play. In the business world, when suppliers negotiate with customers or employees with their managers, fair and comprehensible solutions help ensure stable relationships in the long term.

Negotiation theory distinguishes three main ways to reach a negotiated result:

- o   Cooperative negotiation – e.g., according to the Harvard Method
- o   Fair compromise via equitable distribution
- o   Competitive negotiation – as in traditional marketplace haggling

You can compare the main features of these three negotiation styles, side by side, in the chart that follows. Each of the three has evolved on its own and continues to be used today because of the advantages it offers – with each style offering advantages in different situations, of course. This book focuses on cooperative negotiation – the style that has proven to offer the highest long-term success rate, yielding the results that most satisfy the parties. It is nevertheless important to be familiar with the other two styles as well, since they too are widely used in practice. The competitive style is predominantly used in one-off negotiations, as well as in cases where the balance of bargaining power is highly unequal; a company will also make every effort to come out on top when it is dealing with a competitor.

Another advantage of being familiar with all three styles of negotiation is being able to recognize them when another party tries to employ them – thus allowing you to react accordingly.

	Cooperative negotiation according to the Harvard Method	Fair compromise via equitable distribution	Competitive negotiation / traditional marketplace haggling
Differences are overcome and the gap is closed by...	Asking about the higher goal: "What is really most important to us?"	Mutually exchanging concessions	Exchanging concessions (not always mutually) and the use of tricks and ploys
The opposing party is influenced by...	The use of images and ideas, as well as the eliciting of enthusiasm / identification	Reason	Exploiting bargaining power
Negotiation style employed when...	Long-term cooperation is desired. Note: when the gap is very large, it is easy to end up in a deadlock	Fairness and justice are important to both parties	Our side has more bargaining power – in this case, we come out on top. Note: when the other side has more bargaining power, *they* will end up on top.
Typical tactics	Asking about the other side's needs and interests	Applying criteria that are comprehensible, transparent, and objective	Utilizing concession rules – and sometimes dirty tricks too

CASE STUDY: THE HIGH-SCHOOL REUNION

Nellie's ten-year high-school reunion is coming up, and she is very much looking forward to meeting up with her old friends in Philadelphia again. Everything has been carefully planned – flights and hotels have been booked, meeting points have been arranged, and Nellie has even accepted a dinner invitation from her childhood sweetheart, Tom. She is both excited and nervous. Then, suddenly, Nellie's manager Fleur points out that there is a problem – unfortunately, another member of the team had asked to take a vacation during the same two weeks. The team will be short-handed if both Nellie and Marcus are out of the office at the same time, so management wants one of them to postpone their vacation. Fleur, trying to avoid the tough decision, asks Nellie and Marcus to resolve the situation on their own.

Marcus has booked a Caribbean cruise with his pregnant wife. The couple wants to take their honeymoon before the baby comes. Cruising between the beautiful destinations around the Caribbean will be an unforgettable experience, and this special – non-refundable – offer was too cheap to pass up. Nellie and Marcus decide to meet after lunch to negotiate a solution.

▶ TASK

Broadly sketch out how the discussion might look under each of the three negotiation styles.

► ANALYSIS

1. Cooperative negotiation according to the Harvard Method

The key question here is:

"What is really important to us? What is our ultimate goal?"

a. Both sides want to take their vacation.

b. Both sides want a solution that will allow them to continue working together on amicable terms afterwards.

What are some possible solutions?

a. Asking the team leader to find a suitable temporary replacement for the time they would both be away.

b. Finding some colleague or intern whom they could train to handle the work during their absence.

c. Offering to be available regularly via telephone/internet to respond to anything that may be needed of them while they are on vacation.

2. Fair compromise via equitable distribution

The goal here is to mutually exchange concessions, taking into account fairness and justice.

What are some possible solutions?

a. Have the boss decide upon a solution and assume responsibility for the decision.

b. Marcus and Nellie each take a week of vacation, and the company covers a share of any cancellation or rebooking costs for their travel arrangements.

3. Competitive negotiation / traditional marketplace haggling

Here, each party uses ploys and bargaining power in an effort to get their own way.

What are some possible ways the situation might be resolved?

a. With tears in her eyes, Nellie might allege that she is always the one who has to defer to her coworkers, threatening to quit her job if she can't attend her reunion.

b. Marcus might point out that Nellie recently messed up a big negotiation with an important client – and suggest that giving him preference for the vacation time would be a good way to reward his own recent successful work.

▶ REFLECTION

Which style most appeals to you personally?

Which of the above solutions do you find most realistic?

Expressing yourself clearly and unambiguously

While negotiating, people are constantly listening to what is being said between the lines by the other party. So be careful to avoid "weak" language (e.g., when trying to sell your car, refrain from saying things like, "I'm hoping to get somewhere between $3000 and $4000 – I'm not really very experienced with these sorts of negotiations though...")

Any experienced negotiator will immediately notice if you are unable to express yourself in a strong, clear fashion – and will exploit this to his advantage. Expressing yourself too weakly immediately tells your counterpart that he can whittle away at your opening position quite easily.

SELF-ASSESSMENT 4.2

Take a pen, a piece of paper, and five minutes for the following exercise – enjoy!

► TASK

How would a shrewd negotiator interpret the following statements?

- "We hope that..."
- "Our first offer is..."
- "We're thinking about whether..."
- "We'd be glad if..."
- "We can offer you (*hesitates, looking up into space*)... 65."
- "We'll pay between 60 and 65."
- "What do you think about maybe... 75?"
- "I know it sounds high, but..."

The solution can be found at the end of the chapter.

How to express disagreement skillfully

Why is it important to express your disagreement? Because if you do not, then the other party will assume that you may go along with their proposal, or at least something close to it. So how do you express your disagreement in a professional manner? Simply make it clear to your counterpart that you do not accept his proposal, using both words and body language. Be careful – silence can be construed as consent!

o   Do not object aggressively.
o   Do not respond in an insulting manner.
o   Do not laugh at your counterpart's proposal.
o   Do not be sarcastic.

The correct time to express your rejection of the other side's proposal is immediately after you have heard it. A delayed rejection will often not be perceived as a complete rejection. If several points are being negotiated (e.g., price, delivery terms, payment terms, etc.), then you can decide whether you want to object to each individual item as it is proposed or wait to reject the entire "package".

When negotiating in a team, the rejection of the other side's proposal should always come from the person leading the team. The other members of the team, however, can certainly express their disapproval of the proposal, either through their body language or with a few words to the effect (e.g., "That's definitely outside our budget.")

Why you should take breaks

There are so many good reasons to take brief pauses during the course of your negotiations – yet many negotiators still underestimate the huge benefits that can sometimes be gained from putting a discussion on hold for a bit. People often make hasty decisions, wanting to get their negotiations over with quickly – only to later regret the fact that they accepted a certain result without fully thinking things through.

TIP:
There is a Russian proverb that says: "Morning is wiser than evening."

Here are some of the reasons why people avoid asking for a break while negotiating:

- The other party might see us as weak.
- It's just not normally done during such discussions.
- We'll lose the "flow" of the discussion and lose our momentum.
- Our team always just ends up squabbling when we take breaks during negotiations.
- The other side might get a strategic advantage from being able to talk things over.
- We'll lose valuable time – we want to resolve the issue quickly.

But there are plenty of good reasons to take more pauses than we do. Take breaks when you need them! Here are some of the things you can accomplish during a break in your negotiations:

- Reduce stress, calm down, and gain more time to think things through.
- Review new information or ideas that have been brought up.
- Consult with your team members.
- Keep your supervisor informed about the latest developments.
- Avoid getting stuck in a deadlock.
- Mull over the other party's "final offer".
- Give the other party time to mull over your own "final offer".

Taking breaks in a professional manner

Fleur and Nellie are in Portland to visit a previously unknown supplier who had contacted them with an interesting offer. However, an unexpected piece of information emerges over the course of the contract negotiation – contrary to what the supplier had claimed, they have no experience working with the aerospace industry. Fleur pauses the discussion to ask for a short break. She demonstrates a professional response to the situation – and makes sure that she does not risk agreeing to anything without fully thinking over the matter.

Simply explain why you need to take a break, so that the other side understands. You can skillfully frame it as something that will benefit both parties (e.g., "It'll give both of us a bit more time to think about whether...") Announce that you wish to use the time to consult with the members of your team, then take them into another room and do so. Or else simply think over any newfound information on your own. If necessary, withdraw to a corridor or coffee shop; there may even be a small office or spare conference room that you can use. Inform the other party of how much time you will need and when you will be ready to resume the discussion.

Matters are even easier when you are not negotiating in person – simply schedule another videoconference or inform your counterpart when he can expect to hear back from you by phone or email.

How to make concessions like a seasoned pro

Neil is the youngest of three children. As a child, he quickly discovered that he could get whatever he wanted if he behaved himself nicely. Without even realizing it, he increasingly conformed to his parents' expectations, always getting along well with everyone at home and at school. Now, in his early 30s, he has an interesting job in the aerospace industry. He soon notices that, while negotiating with clients, he repeatedly makes concessions that go beyond the terms that his manager had clearly discussed with him – he gets the sense that he feels pressured to please his clients when they express their dissatisfaction with his proposals. Now he is in a predicament. His clients love his acquiescent nature – but his boss does not, frequently pointing out that "everyone else manages to negotiate tougher." Neil understands that it all goes back to his childhood: he is quick to make concessions because he wants to please others – and this compliance gets him approval and recognition, just like it always has. He knows, however, that he has to learn how to make concessions like a professional, so that he can hold his own even in difficult negotiations.

The art of making concessions in a professional manner is essential to any successful negotiation. Negotiating is all about two parties gradually moving towards each other – and both rigid inflexibility and excessive compliancy impair this process. Thus, the following recommendations:

- Always leave yourself room to make concessions.
- Plan out your concessions beforehand.
- Let the other party make the first concession.
- Actively request concessions from the other party.
- Don't be the first to make a major concession – and object when the other side demands one from you.
- Attach a condition to each concession that you make.
- When you receive a concession from the other party, know that you do not automatically have to make one simultaneously.
- When making concessions that mean little to you, try to get concessions that are important to you in exchange.
- Give concessions incrementally, rather than all at once.
- Give smaller and smaller concessions as the negotiations go on.
- Take advantage of the notion of limited authority. ("That's not a decision that I'm authorized to make here today" or, "Our company policy would require us to have an internal discussion about that first.")
- When negotiating a package deal, remember that absolutely nothing is final until the last point of the package has been agreed upon.

How to tell when the time is right to close the deal

In every negotiation, there comes a time when it seems like you are reaching the end of the line. You often hear lines like: "This is really our final offer" or "I simply can't go any lower". You've gone back and forth with the other party regarding your positions, you've developed solutions, and now all that remains is getting to the final handshake. But how do you know it's really the right moment? And how do you seal the deal?

This also raises the question of whether you should make a "final offer". Be careful! Doing so can be dangerous. Never make a "final offer" unless you can be sure of what you will do if the other party refuses to accept it. Here are some guidelines to follow when making such an offer:

- Express yourself credibly – with regard to both your wording and your body language.
- State your final offer slowly and deliberately.
- Maintain firm eye contact.
- Demonstrate that your entire team is in accordance.
- Demonstrate the finality of the offer (by your tone of voice, by folding your arms, by keeping silent and waiting for a response, etc.)

When the other side makes a final offer, you first need to determine whether it is truly final or whether there might still be some leeway. If it truly does seem to be their final offer, ignore the "finality" and remember what is truly at stake. The right time to close the deal is when the following conditions are met:

- The other side is highly interested.
- A deadline is approaching.
- The gap between the parties has become minimal.
- The other party starts asking implementation-related questions.
- You have made all concessions you could possibly make.

At this point, do the following:

- Take a break to think over the final offer.
- Clarify any important details, in order to avoid unpleasant surprises.
- Have all participants confirm their willingness to agree to the deal.
- Record the agreement in writing.
- Collect your documents, stand up, and part ways with a handshake.

Special case: Building coalitions

After you have successfully mastered one-on-one negotiation, you may wish to take the next step and learn the ropes of multiparty negotiation. In addition to understanding the different roles of team members, there are two more things that you must understand in order to become adept at leading multiparty negotiations:

- The complex interactions between negotiation participants
- The nature of coalition building

The more parties there are in a negotiation, the more complicated the communication becomes. Everyone wants to be heard and understood. The interests of any two parties can be both in harmony and in conflict at the same time, which makes it difficult for a negotiator to figure out how much information to actually reveal. One might have to deal with both cooperative and competitive negotiation styles in rapid succession. The structure and methodology of the negotiations themselves often seem to be the focus of the discussion, even more so than the very matter being negotiated – the person leading the talks will broach the question of how to proceed, everyone will toss out their own ideas, some will be discussed, some will be rejected, but the whole process will require one to spend time and energy on issues that are not even related to the object of the negotiation.

Similarities between one-on-one negotiation and multiparty negotiation

Keep in mind that one-on-one negotiation and multiparty negotiation have more similarities than differences. In both cases, the goal of the parties is to reach an agreement that will send everyone home happy; the basic principles of one-on-one negotiation thus apply to multiparty negotiations as well. The atmosphere of the negotiations is still crucial. Everyone involved will want to have their voices heard. Developing new, innovative solutions continues to be very important. When one party is too inflexible or employs dirty tricks in order to snag a bigger piece of the pie, this is just as damaging in multiparty negotiations as it is in one-on-one negotiations. And the major dilemma of "cooperation versus confrontation" continues to exist, no matter how many parties are involved.

But the balance of power in many two-person negotiations can quickly be altered by the presence of a third party; this is true even if the third party is not involved in the discussion from the start. The third party can be neutral and play a mediating role. Imagine that you are in the process of preparing a prenuptial agreement with your fiancée. In this situation, a lawyer can be brought in to provide advice regarding statutory regulations, without taking sides – both parties benefit from the third party's involvement in this case. However, a third party can just as well be present as an ally to one of the parties. Coalitions can quickly emerge, shifting the balance of power. The coalition-forming negotiations that occur after parliamentary elections in some European countries are a good example of this.

How can multiparty negotiations be defined?

Multiparty negotiations are those that include more than two parties or groups. These can include companies, organizations, countries, or any other interest groups. We are thus speaking here of multilateral discussions, in contrast to bilateral discussions. Multiparty negotiations are distinguished from one-on-one negotiations by the possibilities for coalition-forming, the complexity of the social interactions involved, and the kaleidoscopic structure of the multiparty negotiation process.

The Ham & Egg Company

An enterprising chicken convinces a profit-hungry pig to partner with him to launch a business. "It'll be called HEC – The Ham & Egg Company," says the chicken. "I'll deliver fresh eggs every day, you take care of the ham, and we'll make lots of money!" The pig agrees without thinking... but backs out when he reads the contract!

Before accepting an offer to work together, always check whether it is actually to your advantage. Alliances should not harm anyone – neither the allied parties, nor any third parties. Otherwise, the forming of coalitions will quickly start leaving a bad taste in your mouth.

Coalition building is an interesting aspect of multiparty negotiation. In general, the purpose of forming a coalition is to have a strategic alliance in order to more aggressively pursue common interests. Seemingly weak parties are often unexpectedly strengthened by teaming up with stronger parties, or even with each other. As a result of the accompanying shift in the balance of power, seemingly strong parties then suddenly find themselves facing stronger-than-expected adversaries.

Parties can even continue to form new coalitions at different points in the negotiation process, depending upon the matter being discussed at any particular point in time.

Established coalition strategies

There are two well-known types of coalitions: the *winning coalition* and the *blocking coalition*. In a winning coalition, two separate parties to the negotiation join forces as allies, much like distant enemies in ancient China often allied with each other in order to attack and eliminate a nearby enemy. In a blocking coalition, on the other hand, the parties join together for defensive purposes, for example to prevent a stronger party from achieving his objectives.

How coalitions are formed

In most cases, one party takes the initiative to approach another, suggesting cooperation in order to achieve common goals. For each negotiator, the key questions here are: with whom it is worthwhile to pursue a coalition, on what matters you can cooperate with them, and in what order you will approach these different parties and issues. A variety of criteria can be used to decide with whom and on what issues you will form a coalition, including:

- Similarity of goals or interests
- Similarity of attitudes and values
- Prior experience from past negotiations
- Trust, as well as factors related to power and resources

As soon as a negotiator has decided with whom and on what issues he wishes to pursue a coalition, he must then decide precisely in which order to do so. Every successful affiliation formed between parties will have an immediate effect on the entire system. Other parties will wish to find allies as well, seeking to restore the balance of power in the negotiations.

The way you approach a potential coalition partner is definitely crucial to your success. Any potential partner will ask himself questions like, "Can I really trust them? Will they keep their promises? How will other parties react to our coalition? What long-term effects might there be?" Be sure not to lose sight of the far-reaching implications of forming any particular coalition.

TIP:
Be very careful not to ally yourself with weak parties. Small, powerless partners will not bolster your standing at all – on the contrary, you may unnecessarily weaken your position by affiliating with them. If your coalition partners are not recognized as key decision-makers or are simply dismissed by others as unreasonable, then this will only undermine your own position.

How to dissolve a coalition

As a negotiator, you need to think about how you will manage your coalitions – and also how you will terminate them if circumstances warrant doing so. If a coalition no longer serves your interests, then you can take the opportunity to reach out to new potential partners and form new coalitions. You can also change whatever had motivated your partners to join you in the coalition, making it more attractive for them to seek out new partnerships elsewhere. Imagine that you have partnered with a competitor in order to get a discount from a supplier on the basis of the large quantity that you will purchase together. If your coalition partner decides to drastically lower the amount that they will purchase, then this partnership will no longer be beneficial you, as you will no longer be able to convince the supplier to give you the volume discount. The coalition no longer serves your interests.

One can also sometimes observe mistrust being intentionally sown in order to drive partners to leave a coalition – although this is highly questionable from an ethical point of view and could certainly end up backfiring on a person.

GROUPTHINK ACCORDING TO IRVING L. JANIS

In 1982, researcher Irving L. Janis published a book entitled *Groupthink. Psychological Studies of Policy Decisions and Fiascoes*. The features of group dynamics discussed in this book are relevant to multiparty negotiations:

- Groups tend to develop their own norms and standards that function as expressions of loyalty. Group members who do not conform run the risk of being excluded from the group. Those who are excluded often feel extreme pressure to be accepted back into the group in order to escape their uncomfortable isolation.
- Groups also often develop their own distribution of roles, with both leaders and followers. Other group members play either inhibiting roles, rejecting new ideas, or innovating roles, actively developing such ideas.
- Another risk of groupthink, according to Janis, can be observed in groups that work together over long periods of time. In addition to reduced efficiency, they also demonstrate reduced "reality testing", i.e., a distorted sense of reality. Focusing too much on the skills and climate within their own group and not enough on the critical analysis of new approaches and solutions, they end up overestimating the skills and power of their group and developing

dismissive attitudes towards others. In some cases, the group can become progressively more extreme in its judgments.

It is important for negotiators to be able to deal with the phenomenon of groupthink. The issue of diversity should also be addressed – recognizing differences in culture, status, gender, or age between negotiators can contribute to reducing group conflict. Savvy negotiators will make sure that tolerance and open-mindedness prevail in the negotiating room. A diversity of people and opinions is an enriching – not bothersome – element of a negotiation.

PRACTICE EXERCISE: MILKING TO MOZART

Goal: Build a coalition

For this negotiation exercise, you will need 40 minutes and two motivated fellow negotiators. This is a modified version of an exercise performed by students and executives at Harvard's PON (Program on Negotiation).

▶ THE SITUATION

The EU has recently issued a supplementary budget allocation of €121 millions for a three-nation project dubbed "Milking to Mozart." The idea behind the project is that listening to Mozart makes cows happier and boosts their milk production. As the German farmers' association's official representative, you have traveled to the EU capital of Brussels, where you will meet with representatives of the Spanish and Danish farmers' associations regarding the allocation of the project funds. Your country has sent you to carry out the three-way negotiations, and you are fully authorized to make decisions. In all likelihood, you will never meet with the same two parties again.

If Germany, Spain, and Denmark can reach an agreement regarding how the funds will be divided up between them, then they will share the money accordingly. The exact division of the funds between the three countries is entirely up to them to decide together – however, for statistical purposes, the EU needs to know exactly how much each country will receive. If the three countries cannot reach an agreement regarding the precise allocation of the money for the joint project, then the EU will redirect the funds towards agricultural subsidies for the Baltic states. If only two countries can agree to cooperate, then the EU will allocate a smaller amount to those two countries, as per the table below. In this case as well, the EU would need to know exactly how the funds would be divided up between the two countries – and again, they would accept any division that the countries may agree upon.

Germany alone gets:	€0
Spain alone gets:	€0
Denmark alone gets:	€0
Germany and Spain alone get:	€118 million
Germany and Denmark alone get:	€84 million
Spain and Denmark alone get:	€50 million
Germany, Spain, and Denmark together get:	€121 million

So the three parties can all agree to work together, or any two parties can decide to work together to the exclusion of the third.

The dairy farmers of each country have high expectations of their representatives, each of whom will be participating in such a negotiation for the first time – so each one will do their best to get as much EU funding as possible for their respective countries. The agency in Brussels has set a tight schedule for the talks. The participants have 40 minutes to reach an agreement. If any two of the three participants wish to speak in private, they may do so for up to four minutes, during which the third party may not interrupt them. If an agreement has been reached, it must remain fixed for at least five minutes before it will be considered official. At this point, any two of the three participants can bring the negotiations to a close.

▶ ANALYSIS

After completing the negotiations, discuss your experience, reflecting upon what worked and what could have been handled better.

How are decisions reached in multiparty negotiations?

The multifaceted, unpredictable nature of multiparty negotiations can be compared to the myriad of colorful patterns created by the mirrors inside a kaleidoscope – and the method by which a decision will be reached plays a significant role in the outcome of such negotiations. In one-on-one negotiations, matters are much clearer – either the parties reach an agreement with each other or they don't. In multiparty negotiations, however, the influence of an individual party depends upon how the group has chosen to reach its decision. Here are some of the possibilities:

- *Majority rule*
  More than 50% of votes are needed to take a decision.

- *Weighted majority rule*
  The number of votes per party depends upon certain factors that are known to all parties and can be used as a basis for comparison between them.

- *Majority rule with veto rights*
  The parties reach a decision by majority rule; however, some parties retain the right to veto any decision. In this case, the support of a majority of the parties *and* of all parties holding veto rights are needed for a decision to stand.

- *Consensus rule*
  The parties strive for a unanimous decision, but can accept a large majority if complete unanimity proves to be impossible.

- *Unanimity rule*
  The parties must all agree on a decision unanimously; this is basically how it works in one-on-one negotiations.

- *The Kaldor-Hicks rule*
  This rule compares the sum total of all gains from a decision with the sum total of all losses from a decision. The decision is then taken if all gains from it would theoretically be able to compensate for all losses from it – in theory, this is a highly attractive approach from an ethical perspective. In practice, however, such compensation is, unfortunately, rarely given.

What other possibilities exist besides simply agreeing and disagreeing?

In practice, negotiators have many other choices beyond simply agreeing or disagreeing with a decision. Some possibilities include:

- Abstaining from voting on the decision
- Agreeing with the decision, subject to certain conditions
- Voting against the decision without actively vetoing it
- Making side deals
- Agreeing to partial solutions

Three essential tips for successful multiparty negotiations

- Break complex topics of discussion up into smaller sub-topics. Small workgroups can tackle these in a targeted manner during preliminary discussions.
- Steer the negotiation away from positional bargaining and towards a proper negotiation according to the Harvard Method.
- Keep track of the kaleidoscopic facets of your negotiation and, when moderating the discussions, do not let yourself lose control. The more parties there are in the negotiation, the more important your skills in moderating the group.

SOLUTIONS TO THE SELF-ASSESSMENTS

▶ SELF-ASSESSMENT 4.1

1. Neil is completely taken by surprise – he has no idea what the conversation will be about.
Advice: Ask beforehand!

2. Instead of launching right into it, Dr. Schuster strikes up a friendly conversation. Neil still has no idea what it's all about. ("Mr. Reubens, you've been working with us for two months now – are you happy here?")
Idea: Go along with the small talk, but ask the reason for the conversation if you have not already done so by now. This would be the only way to avoid letting Dr. Schuster exercise too much control right from the outset.

3. Dr. Schuster asks a leading question, to which Neil can only reply "yes". ("Then you're up for a special challenge, right?")
Option: Neil can confirm that he is up for a challenge, but qualify this statement. ("Sure! Let's talk about what that challenge might be though.")

4. Dr. Schuster confronts Neil with lots of facts – and when he supplements these with motivational lines like "I know you can do it!", it becomes nearly impossible for Neil to say no.
Suggestion: Neil could have asked for a bit of time to think things over!

5. Neil's boss dominates him completely, even deciding exactly when the conversation is over. Neil has no chance to refuse.
Tip: Set a time for a follow-up meeting to clarify whatever needs to be clarified!

SOLUTIONS TO THE SELF-ASSESSMENTS

▶ SELF-ASSESSMENT 4.2

Here's what your shrewd counterpart would think about these statements:

"We're hoping for..."
-> You're just "hoping" for that much? Well, then there's definitely plenty room to negotiate!

"Our first offer is..."
-> Great, now let's hear your second offer!

"We're thinking about whether..."
-> Well, keep thinking if you're still not sure!

"We'd be glad if..."
-> Sorry, I'm not here to make you glad!

"We can offer you (hesitates, looking up into space)... 65."
-> No eye contact? Picking a price out of thin air? They're definitely not well-prepared!

"We'll pay between 60 and 65."
-> A range? Great, let's start from 65 and work our way up!

"What do you think about maybe... 75?"
-> Do you really want my opinion?

"I know it sounds high, but..."
-> Is that an apology? If you already know it sounds high, then just make me a better offer!

SUMMARY: BASIC NEGOTIATION TACTICS

▶ **Seven tips**

Mastering basic negotiation tactics will provide you the foundation for being a good negotiator. The study of negotiation involves both theory and practice – the theory provides understanding and knowledge, while the practice trains your actual negotiation skills. Focus on the following seven points as you practice negotiating in the future:

1. Start off like a professional, planning out your goals.
2. First decide on a strategy, then devise your tactics.
3. Avoid expressing yourself too weakly. Be clear and precise.

4. Remember that you can always say no. Express your objections skillfully.
5. Use the power of pauses – take more breaks.
6. Make your concessions like a professional
7. Know the right time to seal the deal.

▶ The kaleidoscopic aspect of negotiations

The more information you need to keep track of (questions, problems, facts, opinions, etc., of each participant in the discussion), the more complex the negotiation becomes. This is the "kaleidoscopic" aspect of negotiations. Recognize the essential role of the agenda and set out clearly what is to be discussed. Tackle discrete issues separately in joint working groups to keep the discussion "tidy".

▶ Multiparty negotiations

An increase in the number of negotiating parties also entails an increase in the risk of communication breakdowns; multiparty negotiations thus need someone to "manage" them. As the person responsible for directing the negotiations, this person should plan out the rules for the discussion, as well as the criteria by which a decision will be taken. He also needs to take into account the unique nature of groupthink and coalition building.

5. THE HARVARD METHOD - *GETTING TO YES*

Cooperative negotiation under the Harvard Method

At the center of the Harvard University campus sits a bronze statue of founder John Harvard, relaxing in an armchair with a book open on his lap. His shoe gleams shinily, having been rubbed by thousands of students for good luck before exams. But even the richest university in the world has not always had luck on its side: The Harvard Management Company, which manages the university's endowment, handled $36.9 billion in funds at the start of the global financial crisis, but lost 22% of this during the crisis. Nevertheless, the university remains world-renowned in both education and research. Among its twelve schools is the famous Harvard Law School, and among the law school's special projects is the Program on Negotiation (PON). Since its founding in 1980, the PON has taken advantage of Harvard's multidisciplinary nature to examine the topic of negotiation from a variety of different perspectives. Among the disciplines represented at the PON are law, psychology, economics, political science, and public relations, as well as international relations. From the very start, the PON's goal has been to incorporate innovative influences into its study of negotiation. In recent years, the program has offered a small number of experienced negotiation professionals the opportunity to participate in a special twice-yearly advanced course on the subject of "Teaching Negotiation in the Organization". This course also addresses the question of why "open negotiation" according to the Harvard Method has become so widely adopted in the field. Among the answers given:

- Few other methods are both so simple and so comprehensive at the same time. The Harvard Method incorporates many other well-known, tried-and-tested approaches and theories.
- The Harvard Method is global in its application – it has proven effective in practice everywhere from the U.S.A. to Germany to China to Russia, independent of any local cultural conditions.

- It has been validated academically – and continues to be developed by the Program on Negotiation.
- The notion of pursuing win-win solutions is ultimately in the interest of all parties. Competitive negotiation is more stressful and more demanding, and someone always ends up losing.
- The Harvard Method's guidelines offer negotiating parties both stability and freedom of action.

SELF-ASSESSMENT 5.1

To get an initial sense of what lies behind cooperative negotiation, take a few minutes to fill out the questionnaire.

▶ TEST: "AM I A COOPERATIVE NEGOTIATOR?"

Criteria	Yes	No
Am I true to myself?		
Do I take a stance?		
Am I unconditionally constructive?		
Do I pursue win-win strategies?		
Do I set realistic negotiation goals?		
Do I know my own interests?		
Am I open to alternatives?		
Am I capable of separating the subject matter from the person when I negotiate?		
Is it easy for me to put myself in someone else's shoes?		
Am I able to accept convincing arguments by other parties?		
Do I readily accept objective criteria as benchmarks?		
Do I truly pay attention to my counterpart?		
Am I an active listener?		
Am I capable of solving conflicts cooperatively?		
Do I handle difficult conversational situations with confidence?		
Am I capable of being consistent in the substance of a negotiation?		
Do I handle my negotiations one step at a time?		

► SOLUTION TO THE SELF-ASSESSMENT

If you checked the "Yes" box for all of the above questions, then you can skip this chapter – if not, then you will find lots of valuable information in the pages that follow.

Negotiate together, instead of against each other

All too often, people seem to think that negotiation is all about "winning", or getting more than the other side gets. But another possibility exists – as the following parable shows.

THE LONG SOUP SPOONS

A young Greek philosopher is on his evening walk, when he meets his teacher. As the two continue walking together, the teacher says, "I visited many places during my years of travel. One day, as I walked through the woods, I heard some horrible moaning sounds. As I continued in the direction from which they came, I saw a large table in a clearing. There was a large pot of steaming hot soup on the table, and all around it stood people with long soup spoons in their hands. Each spoon was as long as the height of the person holding it! The people looked so very hungry. They were trying to eat the soup, but they could not – they were unable to bring the long soup spoons to their mouths. They were so wrapped up in themselves that they took no notice of me. I continued onwards and soon approached another clearing, from which I heard sounds of laughter and mirth. Again I found a table with a pot of steaming hot soup, surrounded by men with long soup spoons – yet the mood here was so different." "Why was it so different?" asked the student. The teacher replied, "Because the men were feeding each other with their spoons."

The above allegory boils the matter down to its essence: working together, instead of against each other, opens up new perspectives. With regard to negotiation in particular, we tend to operate intuitively – negotiating things just as we always have, ever since we were children. In many cases, we are not even aware that there are other, better ways to go about it. And this is where the Harvard Method comes into play, showing us the professional way to negotiate.

The Harvard Method features five principles that take a negotiator step-by-step through the negotiation process. Over the course of this chapter, you will familiarize yourself with these principles. The five steps build upon each other – in other words, the steps must be taken in order, one after the other, just like on a staircase. The five principles of the Harvard Method are:

- Separating the *person* with whom you are negotiating from the *issues* being negotiated, so that you can be soft towards the person and yet hard on the issues.
- Focusing on the interests and motivations of the parties, rather than simply clinging to positions.
- Working together to develop possible solutions that would result in mutual gain – only later evaluating them and choosing one.
- Evaluating options on the basis of fair, objective standards that render any decisions transparent.
- Deciding for or against potential solutions by comparing them against your alternatives.

The consistent application of a win-win strategy results in a systematic shift...		
from:		to:
Positional bargaining	→	Addressing the interests of the parties
"Your problems are your own."	→	"Your problems matter to me too."
"I'll gain control over the other party."	→	"We'll gain control of the process."
Relationships serve as leverage	→	Relationships are stand-alone interests
Concessions lead to a consensus	→	Creativity leads to new solutions
Either a good relationship or a good deal	→	Both a good relationship *and* a good deal
When one side wins, the other side loses (zero-sum game)	→	Both sides win (non-zero-sum game)
Survival of the fittest	→	Fair solutions

Principle #1 of the Harvard Method

Separate the person from the issues – be soft towards the person, but hard on the issues! If you mix personal relationship issues with substantive negotiation problems, then you will both damage the relationship and impede substantive progress in the negotiation. A functional relationship is a prerequisite for efficiently dealing with the substantive issues.

The following advice thus applies:

- Recognize relationship problems, and deal with them separately from the substantive issues of the negotiation.
- Make sure that there is mutual trust, mutual acceptance, and effective communication in your relationship with your counterpart.
- Solve relationship problems *before* you start working on substantive issues.

- Build up mutual trust by always behaving in a trustworthy manner, regardless of your counterpart's behavior.

All of this sounds good in theory, but you may be wondering how it works in practice. And this is a reasonable question – as a negotiator, how can you actually separate the issues from the person? Here are some tips:

- Try to put yourself in your counterpart's shoes.
- Do not presuppose your counterpart's intentions on the basis of your own fears.
- Do not get hung up on assigning blame.
- Work together on solutions, instead of simply submitting unilateral proposals.
- Since both sides want to win, stay on the lookout for face-saving solutions.

When people negotiate, they tend to be focused on themselves. Fleur relates a brief anecdote to Nellie. "My son Manny is in third grade. Yesterday, when he came home from school, he told me about a race in the schoolyard during recess. He told me proudly that he had come in second place, while his biggest rival, a fourth-grade kid named Paul, had come in second-to-last place. I congratulated him and asked him how many kids there had been in the race – and he replied, 'Just me and Paul.' Each and every one of us looks at the world from our own perspective – but when negotiating, true professionals know how to step outside themselves and see things from the perspective of their opponents. To paraphrase the old Native American saying, 'If you want to know your opponent, you must first walk a mile in his moccasins.'"

How to be soft on the person, but hard on the issues

Deal with emotions in a professional manner:

- Do not forget that your counterpart also struggles with his emotions! All negotiators are, first and foremost, human beings.
- You must be able to recognize and understand both your own emotions and your counterpart's emotions. Remember to

articulate your own emotions, and also acknowledge those of your counterpart.
- Avoid reacting with outbursts. Letting go of your emotions in such a manner can lead to emotional counterreactions and sometimes even big arguments. Set a rule that only one person at a time can get worked up. Successfully controlling your outward expression of your emotions is a sign of professionalism.
- Allow your counterpart to let off steam, without allowing yourself to be provoked by this. It will often be easier to discuss things rationally with him afterwards. The best way to proceed is to listen calmly without commenting on his attack, instead just inviting him to continue.
- Symbolic gestures like apologies can go a long way. This is especially true when things are not going well. Invite your counterpart to lunch, for example, or offer him tickets to a trade show.

Communicate in a professional manner:

- Listen actively, without interrupting.
- Ask for clarifications to ensure that you do not miss anything important.
- Sum up what you have understood and confirm whether you have understood correctly.
- Talk about yourself so that your counterpart understands what is important to you; do not strike out at your counterpart.
- Stay calm and serene.

An urban legend tells of a radio conversation that supposedly happened in October 1995 between a U.S. Navy ship and Canadian authorities off the coast of Newfoundland, showing just how tragicomically things might end if one conversation partner insists upon being right and sticking to his guns at all costs.

> American: Please divert your course 15 degrees to the north to avoid a collision.

> Canadian: Recommend you divert YOUR course 15 degrees to the south to avoid a collision.

American: This is the Captain of a U.S. Navy ship. I say again, divert YOUR course.

Canadian: No. I say again, you divert YOUR course.

American: THIS IS THE AIRCRAFT CARRIER USS LINCOLN, THE SECOND LARGEST SHIP IN THE UNITED STATES' ATLANTIC FLEET. WE ARE ACCOMPANIED BY THREE DESTROYERS, THREE CRUISERS AND NUMEROUS SUPPORT VESSELS. I DEMAND THAT YOU CHANGE YOUR COURSE 15 DEGREES NORTH, THAT'S ONE FIVE DEGREES NORTH, OR COUNTERMEASURES WILL BE UNDERTAKEN TO ENSURE THE SAFETY OF THIS SHIP.

Canadian: This is a lighthouse. Your call.

By contrast, the unique tactic of the third U.S. President, Thomas Jefferson, shows how a sound relationship can be established with another party even before the start of a negotiation. Jefferson would first invite his counterpart to his large private library, offering the other a chance to have a look around and perhaps borrow a book. The visitor felt flattered that the president trusted him enough to let him look through his private collection and even borrow something. Jefferson got an opportunity to find out what interested his counterpart – and at the same time, this person was left with an unspoken duty to perform a favor for Jefferson in return.

To encourage your counterpart to change his perceptions, it can be helpful to do something that contradicts his prior experiences. Such an unexpected occurrence can have a powerful effect – as the following example shows:

Brad, a member of Fleur's team, is dissatisfied with his salary and recently had a tense discussion with Fleur about the matter. Two weeks later, Fleur is sitting in the company cafeteria with Nellie once again. "Guess what," says Fleur, "Brad came to speak with me again today. I thought he wanted to give me notice that he was quitting – but it turns out he was just bringing me a box of mini-pastries! I was so surprised!"

BARACK OBAMA SEEKS A NEW DIALOGUE WITH THE ISLAMIC WORLD

On April 6, 2009, U.S. President Barack Obama used a speech before the Turkish parliament in Ankara to send the Islamic world clear signals of rapprochement. "The United States is not, and will never be, at war with Islam," said Obama. Instead, he advocated for a deeper partnership with Muslims, stressing the common struggle against extremists and terrorists who threaten the entire world. Instead of behaving like an adversary, Obama focused on sending peace signals.

Obama, incidentally, earned his law degree from Harvard Law School (as did his wife Michelle). He served as the first African-American president of the prestigious Harvard Law Review and graduated *magna cum laude* in 1991. If you carefully follow his politics, you will continuously encounter the ideas of the Harvard Method.

CASE STUDY: THE CASE OF THE BUDGET CUTS – PART 1

Nellie is very excited – for the first time, she will be handling a difficult negotiation for Fleur. Due to the company's difficult financial situation, the senior management has decided to make cuts affecting a series of budget proposals related to internal communication and motivation. The management would like to reduce the total amount allocated for these proposals from $330,000 to $130,000.

The product management, R&D, and production departments will each have two representatives at the meeting that has been scheduled – the goal of which is to find a way to implement the budget cuts fairly, taking into account the interests of each of the departments.

Representing the product management department on behalf of Fleur, Nellie's goal is to ensure the implementation of as many of the department's budget requests as possible. With the sharp budget cuts, this won't be easy – the other departments will certainly fight for their shares as well. If the three departments are unable to reach a decision jointly, however, management has made clear that they will simply order the cuts themselves. And this would definitely be the worst option – who knows who will get stuck with the biggest cuts? Everyone is tense – they know that the discussions are going to be tough. The day before the meeting, Fleur sits down with Nellie to give her a few tips:

"Don't take your seat right away – put your bag down where you'd like to sit, but then make the rounds. Break the ice with some small talk. Talk about current events, your vacation plans, or what's going on in town. Keep moving – try to greet as many of the participants as possible and engage them in conversation. Pay attention to your posture – both while you're standing and while you're sitting. Avoid being unnecessarily tense or stiff. You can even laugh a bit – it'll help all of you relax. Avoid breaking off into small groups. Remember that it's really annoying when just two people hold the floor in a group of five or more, with everyone else staying on the sidelines. Make sure you involve Stephan and Roberto from R&D as well.

▶ ANALYSIS

Fleur puts Nellie in the mindset to separate the people from the issues, right from the very start. The technique that she suggests to Nellie is called "building rapport."

Building rapport

In the field of communication, *rapport* is understood as a close, empathetic connection with another person, typically reflected in the mirroring of each other's behavior. Get inside your counterpart; enter his worldview. The process of building rapport is called *pacing* – it means that the conversation partners start to mirror each other with regard to their speech, their body language, or even their breathing, in order to establish rapport. Marathoners know "pacers" as runners who maintain a consistent pace, helping others to ensure a steady rhythm and complete the race within their target time. In the context of negotiation, you can be a "pacer" by means of:

- *Verbal pacing* – Express yourself in the same manner as your conversation partner – this can include visual, auditory, and kinesthetic "language". You can also mirror the tone, volume, and rhythm with which he speaks.

- *Pacing of postures, gestures, and facial expressions* – If your counterpart wants some distance and leans back, then you lean back as well. If he leans forward, then you do the same. Take on the same posture as your counterpart and mirror his gestures and facial expressions. Pacing experts even manage to adopt the same breathing rhythm as their conversation partners.

- *Leading* – In this case, you take the lead, steering your conversation partner in a particular direction – for example, by changing your own posture or speech patterns. If rapport has been established, then your conversation partner should follow your lead. Leading should not be manipulative, but rather should be done in a respectful manner to set a conversation on a new course (for example, moving from the problem towards the solution, or from an angry mood to a calmer one).

CASE STUDY: THE CASE OF THE BUDGET CUTS – PART 2

Nellie calls Fleur on her cell phone. "Fleur, what should I do? We just took a ten-minute coffee break – but everyone's beating up on each other in here. Things started off well, but then the guys from production just went on the attack. Then R&D started sniping back, of course – and things went completely out of control from there."

"It's good that you called, Nellie," replies Fleur. "Now, keep calm! Listen, the problems here are relationship problems. Relationship problems can be disturbing because of the gap between your expectations and your actual experience with the other negotiators. The best way to fix a relationship problem is to mention it directly – though not in a way that generates resistance from the others." "Yes, yes," Nellie interrupts, a bit stressed out. "I know you're right. It sounds so simple. But what should I actually do now?"

Fleur continues, "Respond by addressing the fact that attacking others is inappropriate, because it only results in counterattacks. Suggest that you will sketch out your thoughts on a flipchart. First, outline the budget allocations that everyone is voluntarily willing to strike out – this will provide a chance to achieve some small initial success. Introduce a rule for the discussions: 'Face the problem, not the people.' You will all listen to each other with open minds – none of the same old stories. And listening does *not* simply mean keeping your mouth shut as you wait impatiently for the other person to finish talking so that you can take the floor once again. Let your heads deal with the issues and your hearts deal with the people! And in order to accomplish this, each of you needs to let go of your focus on yourselves and instead be open and receptive, trying to understand the others rather than judge them. Nellie, remember: *soft on people, hard on points* – "S.O.P.H.O.P." is how my professor at Harvard drilled it into our heads. At the time, I had to write this on a small card that I would look at before every negotiation! Anyway, I'm sure you'll manage to create an atmosphere that will be conducive to a good result. Call me if there's anything else you need."

In the case study, Fleur makes clear to Nellie that she can still be hard on the points while being soft towards the people. It helps to sit side-by-side at the table, in front of the contract or drawings or whatever other documents are being discussed, in order to work towards a solution together – the physical reinforces the psychological. Speak matter-of-factly with your counterparts about what is happening in the negotiation and how they feel about it. It's not the end of the world to say something like: "You know, my people feel like they've been treated poorly and they're very angry about it. Even if we could actually come to an agreement, we're afraid that it probably wouldn't hold up. Are your people getting the same impression?" This will generally result in the negotiations becoming more active and focused on the problem at hand, as the participants free themselves from the burden of repressed emotions.

Also helpful, of course, are the following tips already discussed in earlier chapters:

- Be clear about your goals (maximal/realistic/minimal).
- Be clear about your negotiating room.
- Be well-prepared in general.
- Be clear about your BATNA.
- Improve your BATNA whenever possible.

Principle #2 of the Harvard Method

Focus on interests, rather than positions. Behind every position, there is some sort of interest, need, or motivation – the idea that legitimately drives the negotiator. Different interests can usually be satisfied several different ways – interest-oriented negotiation is thus more "open" than position-oriented negotiation with regard to possible outcomes and, as such, allows for more new solutions to be developed. Although taking up a position can highlight one's strengths, it can also reveal one's weaknesses when one's demands are not met – and there is always the risk of losing face.

Thus, the following recommendations:

- Be clear about your own interests and state them openly, without actually taking up a position.
- Try to figure out the interests behind the other party's position. ("Why do you need...?")
- Bring up any ideas you may have that could advance the parties' interests.
- Focus on shared interests to start, leaving conflicting interests to the side for the time being.

At this point, we need to explain the terms "position" and "interest", as used in the context of negotiation. Imagine the following situation: Shortly before Easter, two children are arguing with each other. "I need four eggs, I want to decorate them for Easter," says the boy. The girl replies, "But there are only four eggs left, and I need all four of them to bake something." "But I called them first!" "It doesn't matter – we'll split them evenly." "But two eggs aren't enough, I need all four!" Their mother then intervenes – and she has dealt with such situations many times before. She starts off by asking the children what they want to do with the eggs. "I want to paint them and bring them to school," says the boy. "I want to bake hot cross buns," says the girl. Each of the children has made their position clear – they each "need four eggs". Without knowing the interests behind their positions, the best-case result might be dividing the eggs up evenly – and in the worst case, one of the children would end up with none. But after the children's interests have been clarified, a better solution appears. The girl's interest is in baking a cake, so she needs the egg whites and yolks. The boy's interest is in painting the eggs, so he needs only their shells. While their positions put them in conflict, their interests can both be achieved together by blowing out the eggs – leading to a solution in which both of them "win". Do you think this doesn't work in real-life negotiations? You may be familiar with the following historical example:

THE SINAI PENINSULA

In 1967, during the Six-Day War, the Sinai Peninsula was occupied by Israel. In 1978, Egypt and Israel came to Camp David for peace talks. Israel insisted on continued control over the peninsula, while Egypt did not want to give up even a centimeter of the territory. Several new maps were drawn up, each proposing new borders.

U.S. President Jimmy Carter mediated between the two negotiating teams, which were headed by Israeli Prime Minister Menachem Begin and Egyptian President Anwar Sadat. Carter eventually put forward the crucial question of the parties' interests.

For Egypt, it was all about getting back a piece of territory that, despite past occupations by the Greeks, Romans, Turks, French, and British, had been theirs even in the times of the pharaohs. For Israel, however, it was not about the land – all they wanted was security, and they needed to prevent any possibility of Egypt lining up tanks along their border once again to attack them.

The solution was that the peninsula would be returned to Egypt, but that they would leave the territory demilitarized. Egypt could again fly their flags over the Sinai and save face in the Arab world, while Israel could feel secure with no Egyptian tanks coming close enough to attack them. In March 1979, the two parties signed the Egypt-Israel peace treaty. Sadat and Begin were awarded the Nobel Peace Prize as recognition of their efforts in working towards reconciliation. After the end of his presidency, Jimmy Carter founded the Carter Center, a non-profit organization focused on human rights and international mediation; he too received a Nobel Peace Prize in 2002 for his work.

CASE STUDY: THE CASE OF THE BUDGET CUTS – PART 3

Fleur's phone rings – it's Nellie again. *Strange, she should still be busy with the negotiation*, thinks Fleur. She answers the phone.

"Fleur, I'm in the bathroom, so I can't speak very loudly," whispers Nellie, "Anyway, the mood in the room is fine now, but no one is willing to budge on anything. No one will say what's most important to them or why. Everyone just wants to strip away the other departments' budget allocations – and they protest if anyone mentions cutting their own department's proposals. We're starting to just go around in circles. What should I do now?"

"Listen," says Fleur. "Remind them of that fact that the worst outcome for everyone involved would be management unilaterally deciding what to cut. Then start asking questions. Ask lots of questions – questions that get right to the root of what each department's interests are, like 'What's ultimately most important for you?' Then ask questions that really get at what's behind the positions they've taken: 'What's the benefit of this?' 'Why do you need that?' And don't forget to put our own interests out there. Our most important concern right now is getting the new Smartphones for the department staff, so that you all have access to company data at all times. We'd be okay not going through with the Easter promotion though." Fleur hears the restroom door open, as Nellie whispers her thanks and hangs up.

How to find out the other party's interests

In the case study, Fleur's advice to Nellie is to ask, ask, ask. Indeed, asking open-ended questions is the most effective technique for finding out and understanding another party's interests. The following sorts of questions lend themselves to this process:

- General direct questions regarding the other side's interests:
    - What are your ultimate goals from this negotiation?
    - What is your main concern?
    - What interests of yours lie behind this concern?
    - What would happen if...?
    - What would happen if not?

- Questions regarding the interests behind specific positions:
    - What exactly is important to you about...?
    - What do you gain if you get...?
    - What would... enable you to accomplish?
    - Why do you need...?

At the same time, you should be sure to make your own interests known to the others; you can use the following lines:

- For me, what's important is...
- I would like to achieve... because...
- I'm worried about the fact that...
- What I hope is to...
- My biggest concern is...

The following conversation between Neil and Nellie demonstrates what happens when parties insist on sticking to their positions, without trying to understand the other side:

> NEIL: The apartment needs to be renovated; we really need to put a new floor in. We should go for some nice

parquet flooring. I like smoked oak – it's got a really nice color and it'd go well with our sofa.

NELLIE: But it would cost way too much for our budget. Our monthly expenses are so high!

NEIL: Our monthly budget has been stable for a while now. We're getting by just fine.

NELLIE: No, our expenses are still too high to start splurging on expensive flooring.

NEIL: A young couple like us needs to invest in good décor.

NELLIE: A young couple like us can't afford such expensive things!

NEIL: When people like you go around in high heels all the time, that really puts a lot of stress on a floor.

NELLIE: You really need to think about what's important in our relationship.

NEIL: You're so cold and distant – you don't care about what's important to me.

NELLIE: I'm a very considerate partner – who knows how to live within her means!

What do you think – will Nellie and Neil manage to see eye to eye? What could help them reach some sort of agreement? Each one putting themselves in the other's shoes. (Though this doesn't literally mean that Neil should put himself in Nellie's high heels!) People often see only the merits of their own position – and simply see their counterpart as wrong. But if you want to influence someone, then you need to understand their perspective. Understanding the other often leads one to rethink one's own views – which reduces the potential for conflict. People tend to assume that whatever they fear is what their counterpart intends to do. This results in them interpreting everything their counterpart says in the most negative way possible, always presuming the worst intentions. In many cases, people immediately reject any new ideas brought up by their counterpart – ideas which may actually have been good for everyone involved. If Nellie had reacted in an unexpected way, for example, searching for ways to understand Neil's point of view instead of letting herself get provoked, then the conversation above could have played out differently.

Be careful with blame

Do not blame the other party for their problems. Even if an accusation is justified, it will usually be counterproductive anyway. The other party will feel like they are being attacked. They will get defensive – and won't listen openly anymore.

Only when you know and understand the other parties' interests – and your own interests are also known and understood by them – should you proceed to the next step: developing solutions.

Principle #3 of the Harvard Method

Develop as many potential solutions as possible, together with the other parties – though only later should you evaluate them and decide! Finding the optimal solution that will best serve everyone's interests requires the creative brainstorming of everyone involved. In order for creativity to flow as well as possible, hasty judgments and firm stances should be avoided. Search for something beyond "the" correct solution. Free yourself from any notions that the "pie" is limited or that everyone should just worry about solving their own problems.

Here are some suggestions:

- Pose "creative questions" (open-ended questions geared towards discovering possible solutions).

- Do not be satisfied with the first good solution that you find – rather, continue brainstorming for more possibilities or variations.
- Seek solutions that take into account the interests of both parties – i.e., solutions that advance the other party's interests as well.
- Hold off on accepting or rejecting any possible solutions until the creative potential of all participants has been exhausted.

THE EGG OF COLUMBUS

In the late 15th century, many people still believed that the earth was flat – and that if you kept going far enough in any direction, eventually you would plunge off the edge into nothingness. Only slowly were people starting to get used to the crazy notion of a sphere-shaped earth.

A certain Christopher Columbus was ahead of his time. "If the earth is a sphere," he reasoned, "then it must be possible to circumnavigate it in either direction. So if I continue sailing westward, then I will find another route to India." The idea was revolutionary at the time, and people did not believe him. Columbus asked the Spanish king for money to equip a fleet. The king consulted with his advisors, who simply shook their wise heads. They were of the opinion that it was no use throwing money away on such a crazy venture. But Columbus was a man of action – tough yet flexible in his approach. He asked the queen Isabella of Castilia for support, she granted it, and on August 3, 1492, he sailed off with just three ships. After weeks at sea, doubts started to emerge – there had still been no sight of land. But then, on October 12, the long-awaited shouts finally rang out: "Land! Land!"

When Columbus returned home, he was celebrated as a hero. But the king's advisors were not quite pleased. During a dinner at the house of Cardinal Mendoza, his greatest adversary, Columbus was told that his discovery of the "New World" was no great feat, as someone else would have discovered it eventually. In response, Columbus asked everyone present to try standing a boiled egg on its end. They all tried, unsuccessfully. "It's impossible – try it yourself!" they challenged Columbus. Columbus then took the egg, tapped it gently on the table to slightly dent its shell, and then successfully stood the egg on its end. When the others protested that they could have done just the same, Columbus replied, "That, gentlemen, is the difference– while you *could* have done it, I actually *did* it!"

The above anecdote demonstrates that it is worthwhile to believe that solutions exist, even if this seems impossible at first glance. Negotiators often think only "inside the box", as their own personal shallow pool of experiences limits the sorts of possibilities that they can imagine.

Incidentally, another version of the Columbus story circulates in South America, in which he does not break the egg on the table, but rather stands the egg on its end in a pile of salt – which just goes to show that there's always more than one solution to any problem!

How to generate options when negotiating

One of the basic ideas of negotiating for mutual benefit (the "mutual gains approach") is the notion that the "pie" can be enlarged. Use brainstorming to search for solutions – a group of brains will generate more ideas than one alone. Here are some recommendations:

- Quantity before quality – anything goes. The goal at this stage is simply to come up with as many "options" as possible. (Options are *potential* solutions, not actual solutions.)
- Write all options down. (Any option that is only spoken will quickly be forgotten.)
- Do not evaluate the different potential solutions until the next stage. (No "killer phrases" or discussions that take you away from the actual task at hand at this stage – simply collecting ideas.)

CASE STUDY: THE CASE OF THE BUDGET CUTS – PART 4

Fleur is at home, getting ready to eat dinner with her family. Her cell phone rings – it's Nellie again. "Good evening, Fleur," says Nellie. "We've just finished up – and I wanted to get back to you about how the rest of the meeting went." It is clear from Nellie's voice that she is now relaxed, though exhausted. "Anyway, in a nutshell: We managed to split up the budget cuts fairly, in a way that satisfied everyone. I'll quickly go through all of our positions. One: We've cancelled the fancy Christmas party plans with the celebrity chef. Two: We're going to split up the employees for the customer orientation training – some of the staff will take the training this year and the rest will take it next year. Three: With regard to the laser copier, it looks like we're only going to order one instead of two, and we're going to share it with the HR staff. Four: I managed to make sure we'll get the Smartphones, though we're only going to lease them instead of buying them. Anyway, we got creative and worked out the kinks. Being able to visualize things on the flipchart really helped a lot, as did going through all the possibilities before we analyzed them. R&D and Production also came out of the meeting with similar results. You'll see all the details tomorrow morning. Thanks for all your help today!"

Principle #4 of the Harvard Method

Insist upon the use of fair, objective standards and procedures. You will achieve fair and reasonable results from your negotiations if the path towards the decision is transparent. If the decision-making criteria, as well as the decision-making procedures, are accepted by both sides, then neither party will feel like the decision was arbitrary.

Look for generally accepted rules, norms, values, and legal principles that can be applied as objective decision-making criteria. They should:

- be independent of any partisan interests of individual participants in the negotiations,
- have authority by virtue of being applicable to all participants,
- enable standardization for future negotiations,
- have the potential to be used in other situations with other parties in other places.

How to bring legitimation into play

The more neutral the standards used (rules, accepted guidelines, etc.), the less the risk of parties feeling poorly treated or later trying to go back on their agreement. The objective criteria should be equally applicable to both sides; you can use a reversal test to check this. For example, if a real estate trader wants to buy your house and presents you a standard form, a savvy thing to do would be to ask whether he uses the same form when he sells a house too.

Legitimation must be insisted upon. Get used to searching for objective criteria, together with the other party, for resolving each instance of dispute. Insist upon applying these criteria – and be flexible enough yourself to accept reasonable proposals that the other party may make in this regard.

Here are some ways to ask directly about criteria, i.e., about benchmarks that your counterpart would accept:

- What would you consider a good benchmark here?
- As far as you're concerned, what would make our outcome here fair?
- How did you come up with these criteria?
- Can you tell me how you came to that conclusion?

And here are some ways to introduce your own benchmarks:

- I could go along with your proposal if...
- Would you accept this offer if you were in my shoes?
- In a similar situation...
- In our company/industry, usually...

Examples of objective criteria

- Expert knowledge (e.g., scientific studies, expert opinions and analyses)
- Precedents (similar previous cases that can be used as benchmarks for comparison of procedures)
- Moral criteria (such as reciprocity, equality, etc.)
- Court decisions
- Traditions (i.e., common practice, customs, history, culture)

KING SOLOMON'S JUDGMENT

The reign of King Solomon is portrayed in the Bible as a time of peace and well-being. When Solomon was granted a wish by God, he asked for the wisdom to govern his people justly. God granted him this request.

One day, two young women came before the king seeking justice. One of them said, "Pardon me, my lord. This woman and I live in the same house, and I had a baby while she was there with me. The third day after my child was born, this woman also had a baby. We were alone; there was no one in the house but the two of us. During the night this woman's son died because she lay on top of him. So she got up in the middle of the night and took my son from my side while I was asleep. She put him by her breast and put her dead son by my breast. The next morning, I got up to nurse my son – and he was dead! But when I looked at him closely in the morning light, I saw that it wasn't the son to whom I had given birth." The other woman said, "No! The living one is my son; the dead one is yours." But the first one insisted, "No! The dead one is yours; the living one is mine." And so they argued before the king.

Then the king said, "Bring me a sword." So they brought a sword for the king. "Cut the living child in two and give half to one and half to the other." The woman whose son was alive was deeply moved out of love for her son and said to the king, "Please, my lord, give her the living baby! Don't kill him!" But the other said, "Neither I nor you shall have him. Cut him in two!" Then the king gave his judgment: "Give the living baby to the first woman. Do not kill him; she is his mother."

What does this example show? King Solomon opted for a decision-making process that seemed drastic at first, saying that he would cut the child in half. This process was challenged on moral grounds by the child's mother, whose love went beyond mere "possession" of the child. An impartial third party, King Solomon made his decision based on moral criteria.

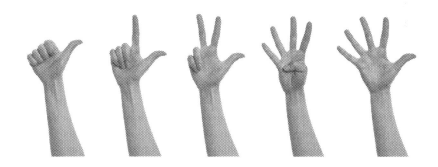

One cuts, the other chooses

Can you recall some situation in your childhood when there was just one portion of cake, for example, for you and your sibling to share – and each of you were worried that you would end up with the smaller piece? Perhaps your mother came up with a Solomonic solution: one sibling would cut it in two, and then the other could choose which piece they wanted. This way, no one could complain that they were being treated unfairly.

When it comes to such processes, it is important that there be transparency for everyone involved. Imagine that you find out one day that you have inherited a mansion full of antiques from a rich aunt – but you will share the inheritance equally with your two brothers and eight cousins. There are several possible ways for the executor of the will to make a fair distribution here. He can define eleven equal portions and let everyone choose lots at random, thus giving everyone an equal chance. He can also simply sell everything and distribute the proceeds equally. Or he can let the nephews and nieces themselves split the estate into eleven portions and then choose. Or... well, as you can see, even the decision-making procedures themselves need to be planned out in such a way that conveys a sense of justice to everyone involved. Otherwise, all the nephews and nieces would start quarreling over the inheritance – and a judge would end up simply deciding everything by decree.

CASE STUDY: CREDIT INSURANCE SAVES THE DAY

Florian, Fleur's husband, owns a medium-sized plastics company called Polyflo, specializing in the manufacture of automotive components. Since he is not currently utilizing the full extent of his production capacity, he is on the lookout for another contract in the passenger car segment. He can hardly believe his luck when, at a trade fair, he is presented with the possibility of a huge contract with a major automotive supplier. After some lengthy discussions, the two sides finally reach agreement on a million-dollar deal. Florian bulks up his machinery, rents an extra warehouse, and hires 15 new employees. The financial press is constantly talking about the ruinous auto price wars, but he scarcely pays any attention – he's got the contract in his pocket.

Then Florian finally starts seeing the signs of the financial crisis, as his powerful business partner goes into a financial tailspin. Payments are never made for the goods that Polyflo delivers. One day, Florian finally hears the news: the big automotive supplier has filed for bankruptcy. Florian himself is deep in debt at this point, as a result of his new investments and ongoing costs, which he now can no longer afford. Will Polyflo go bankrupt too? No – fortunately, Florian has taken out credit insurance. By undertaking some restructuring as well, he can save Polyflo from collapse. But his exact claim for compensation is still to be negotiated. Florian meets with Paul Lissy from the insurance company.

MR. LISSY: We've investigated your case and we've determined that you have a claim, in the amount of two million dollars.

FLORIAN: I see. And how did you reach this number?

MR. LISSY: We decided that that's what your company is currently worth.

FLORIAN: I understand, but on what basis did you make this determination?

MR. LISSY: Why? How much did you think your company was worth?

FLORIAN: As much as I'm covered for.

MR. LISSY: The coverage depends entirely upon the company's structure and revenues.

FLORIAN: Over the last five years, we've taken in $14.5 million per year, on average. So based on your own terms, the indemnity should be at least $3 million.

MR. LISSY: That's too much. Everyone's trying to get money now – all these small companies with no equity.

FLORIAN: One of our competitors, Polyfix, recently got four million from you. And they're smaller than us. I'm sure you would agree that I should get as much as is necessary in order to save my company – that's what we contracted for. I'm not asking for 3, 4, 5 million; I'm just asking for a fair determination of the indemnity.

MR. LISSY: Okay, I can offer you $3.5 million – that's the maximum amount possible under our company policy.

FLORIAN: Where does your company get that number?

MR. LISSY: Wow, you really don't give up. Listen, $3.5 million is the max I can give you. Take it or leave it,

FLORIAN: Maybe $3.5 million is fair. I don't know. And I understand that you're bound by company policy. But as long as you can't objectively tell me exactly how you got that number, I'm going to have to get in touch with an expert. Why don't we speak again tomorrow morning? Would ten o'clock work for you?

The next day, after getting some sound advice from a plastics industry expert, Florian agrees to accept compensation in the amount of $3.8 million.

One can also see the importance of negotiating with uniform standards when one purchases from Europeans as an American, or vice versa. Converting between the metric system and ounces or gallons can easily lead to errors. This can be downright fatal if, for example, a valuable spacecraft is involved (see below).

Agree upon uniform standards together with your counterpart; this can help avoid (sometimes expensive) misunderstandings.

THE LOSS OF THE MARS CLIMATE ORBITER

Mars, the red planet, is Earth's neighbor in the solar system – and is quite similar to Earth in many ways. Planetary researchers have always been fascinated with it and continue to send probes and robots to explore its every detail. Does it hold water – or even life? How is the weather there? On December 11, 1998, NASA launched a probe named the Mars Climate Orbiter, which was to orbit the planet gathering climate and atmospheric data. The launch went off without a hitch, as did the long journey to Mars. On September 23, 1999, the Mars Climate Orbiter reached its destination.

While slowing down the probe, it was also necessary to avoid allowing it to dip too deeply into Mars' atmosphere – or else it could burn up. The maneuver had worked fine on other missions. But the Mars Climate Orbiter went out of radio contact when it passed behind Mars, and communication was never reestablished. The $200 million probe was lost. Instead of passing by Mars at a distance of 150 kilometers, the orbiter had been on a path that would have taken it within 57 kilometers of the surface – and at this distance, it would have disintegrated due to atmospheric stresses.

The embarrassing cause of the navigation error was soon discovered. As usual, NASA had undertaken its calculations in meters and kilometers – but one piece of ground software, supplied by Lockheed Martin, had performed calculations using American measurement units. Nobody had noticed the discrepancy. As a result, the trajectory of the probe was miscalculated. It came too close to Mars and was lost – as the rest of the world shook their heads in astonishment.

Principle #5 of the Harvard Method

Decide for or against a negotiated agreement only after comparing it against your best alternative! A negotiation can be considered successful if it gives you a result that is better than the best alternative you have available elsewhere. No one would agree to a negotiated outcome when they have another course of action that is better. And when you have such an alternative, you avoid feeling dependent upon your counterpart in the negotiations.

Here are some recommendations:

- Work out in advance all possible external alternatives to the best possible negotiation result.
- Then, only agree to a negotiated result if it is better than any of your alternatives.
- Check whether the other side has any better alternative to a proposed agreement.
- Do not threaten your counterparts with their lack of alternatives. Rather, simply make clear to them the decision-making problem that they face.
- During the course of the negotiation, bring up each party's second-best alternative as an option.

Principle #5 of the Harvard Method is so important that it could even be considered Principle #0. The other four principles follow the course of a negotiation chronologically, but this fifth principle is independent. Even before entering into a negotiation, one needs to know what alternatives he has in case the negotiations yield nothing. The acronym BATNA (best alternative to a negotiated agreement) is widely known and used in the

English-speaking world – you might even be asked directly about your BATNA. (see chapter 2)

When reaching a point where an agreement seems unlikely, your focus should no longer be on what you might get from the negotiation, but rather on your alternatives. Everything else should be compared against your BATNA. And the better your BATNA, the greater your negotiating power.

A common psychological problem involves "summing up" one's alternatives – saying, for example, "If I can't reach an agreement with this investor, then I can always handle production on my own, sell intellectual property rights, grant licenses, and so on." One then might calculate that the *sum* of all these possibilities is more attractive than the expected outcome of the negotiations – forgetting that one will only be able to realize a *single* alternative outcome.

CASE STUDY: SEBASTIAN'S WATNA

Neil, Sebastian, and Leon went to college together and have stayed in touch; they meet up once a month at a local bar. Sebastian returned to the U.S.A. four months ago after a year of traveling around South America. He is monitoring every major online job board and has applied to more than 30 new positions since returning, but has not yet had any luck. His initial eagerness is starting to wear off as he grows increasingly frustrated. He tells Neil and Leon about an interview in which the following conversation took place:

HR MANAGER: Mr. Stanislawski, you've been job searching for a while now. I presume this means you're quite flexible at this point?

SEBASTIAN: Yes, of course.

HR MANAGER: So, you'd be willing to work some weekends too when things get busy around here?

SEBASTIAN: Sure.

HR MANAGER: Excellent. And do you drive?

SEBASTIAN: Yes, I have a car.

HR MANAGER: Great, then you'd be able to drive out to meet some clients occasionally. It won't be too often though...

Sebastian finds himself in an uncomfortable negotiating position here. His BATNA is not very good – if he walks away, he remains unemployed. In a way, he has no BATNA – only a WATNA (worst alternative to a negotiated agreement). His negotiating position is very weak because he has no real alternative. The HR manager knows this – and takes advantage of it.

"Hmmm," Leon chimes in. "You know, I got a call from a headhunter last week. He's looking for a patent lawyer for a pharmaceutical company, and they felt I was the most qualified candidate. I decided to go for the interview – I figured at least I can test my market value. I told them straight up that I don't really want to leave Seattle. Asked them all about flexible schedules and about what kind of company car I could get."

Leon has a very strong negotiating position. He has a very attractive BATNA – he can simply remain at his current job.

An intensive analysis of your alternative courses of action, should a negotiation fail, can often greatly increase your bargaining power. Your most attractive alternatives are typically not the most obvious ones. You need to figure out what they are – and this should happen *before* the actual negotiation.

Proceed as follows:

- Come up with a list of actions that you would take if the negotiations yield no results.
- Choose the most promising ideas on this list and develop them into practical options.
- Pick the best of these options and start undertaking preparatory steps – carry out preliminary discussions, build coalitions, or even negotiate with other parties.

Sebastian could have created a list of potential job openings. He could have thought about whether he would be prepared to move to another city, seek the support of a career coach, or become self-employed. The possibility of self-employment could have been fleshed out even further. The more detailed his alternative courses of action, the more bargaining power he was likely to have. It is important to note that all of these actions should have taken place *before* his job interview.

Incidentally, it is also much easier to break off negotiations if you know how you will then proceed. The stronger your readiness to allow the negotiations to fail, the more powerfully you will be able to represent your own interests in the discussions. This insight is put into action even at the highest international level – as the following story shows.

OBAMA'S CUBAN REVOLUTION

On April 9, 2009, the *Süddeutsche Zeitung* ran an editorial that stated: *"Ten U.S. Presidents have played tough with Fidel Castro. They wanted to march into Cuba and oust its dictator or bring him down via the trade embargo. They all failed. Now, Barack Obama is trying to handle things his own way. Although he has not lifted the embargo, he has loosened its shackles considerably – and this is precisely what may lead to a change in Cuba."*

To this question of whether the U.S. government's new strategy is the right one, political scientist Thomas Risse, professor of international politics at the Freie Universität Berlin, replies: *"It's at least an overdue change of direction. They've done the wrong thing for a long time, with harsh sanctions that only fed Cuba's national propaganda. They deprived themselves of the possibility of having positive influence. Now, things are on a human level once again."*

Obama has strategically worked on improving his own possibilities, while simultaneously weakening his opponent's BATNA.

If Cuba declines the U.S. attempts at rapprochement, then everything stays the same in the country. Thus, Cuba does not really have much of a BATNA. Cooperation, on the other hand, would bring great benefits – Florida is so close, and the U.S. government has already started easing travel restrictions and taking the first steps towards a renewal of trade relations. Despite the embargo, the U.S. has been, and will continue to be, Cuba's most important source of foreign currency. Although some easing of the embargo was expected, the U.S. government's announcement that American telephone companies can work directly with Cuban partners was a surprise. This should foster communication between the countries, further stimulating the Cuban people's desire for change. Bringing about change through a series of small steps is nothing new – decades ago, the Cold War ended the same way. From this perspective, President Obama is working on several levels for the long-term expansion of possibilities for the U.S. By getting even the Cuban people on his side, he increases the pressure on the Cuban government to cooperate. The U.S.'s rapprochement will pose new challenges to Cuba's socialist government, which – without the U.S. as an "enemy" – will have a harder time explaining to the Cuban citizens their lack of freedom and prosperity.

And how did Fidel Castro respond to all this? *"Cuba has resisted and it will continue to resist,"* he announced. But for the moment, he is alone in this stance; his brother and successor, Raul Castro, has initially said nothing of the sort.

The Harvard Method is the classic negotiation strategy. Researchers from Harvard University have spent many years observing and analyzing the most varied sorts of negotiations – from collective bargaining to everyday problems – and have derived five principles to which every successful negotiator should adhere.

▶ The goal of the Harvard Method

The goal of the Harvard Method is proper, open negotiation. It's not about whether you should be "hard" or "soft" in your negotiation – rather, it is about being both hard *and* soft: hard on the issues and soft (i.e., friendly) towards the person. Each side can still look the other in the eye afterwards, without feeling like they've been ripped off. Instead of "survival of the fittest", the two sides work towards solutions from which both of them benefit. This is the most successful strategy in the long term.

▶ Principle 1: Separate the person from the issues.

When you mix substantive issues with personal issues, it becomes difficult to make progress in a negotiation. This principle builds upon a fundamental notion from communication psychology – namely, that two people can only reach good substantive solutions when the relationship between them is intact. Fixing relationship problems always takes precedence over substantive issues. Building trust is especially important in the context of negotiations.

▶ Principle 2: Focus on interests, rather than positions.

It is essential for negotiators to understand the difference between interests and positions. Positions often conflict (e.g., dollar values in salary negotiations). Interests are what truly motivate a negotiator (such as career growth or stable employment). In many cases, the interests of parties to a negotiation are not obvious, but rather must be probed out – the key lies in knowing what questions to ask.

▶ Principle 3: Develop options first, evaluate them later.

Once the parties' interests are out in the open, the next step is to increase the size of the "pie". Many negotiations stick to well-trodden paths and consider only a few basic options – but creativity is truly necessary here. The potential solutions should take into account the interests of all parties.

▶ Principle 4: Insist upon the use of objective standards and procedures.

Everyone has different standards. Sometimes, these standards are treated as absolutes – and this leads to huge difficulties in a negotiation, with both sides arguing over which standards are the "right" ones. Thus, you should seek generally applicable rules, values, or principles that can be used as objective decision-making criteria. These rules should be acknowledged and recognized by all parties during the course of the negotiation.

▶ Principle 5: Make a decision based on comparison with your best alternative.

Many negotiators have difficulty with their decisions towards the end of a negotiation, simply because they did not think through their best alternative prior to the negotiation. A negotiation is only a success if its outcome is better for you than your best alternative outside the context of the negotiation. Threatening the other party on the basis of their best alternative demonstrates a lack of tact.

▶ An important closing note

The Harvard Method is a holistic approach; the individual principles build upon one another. They make sense together, rather than in isolation. And simply reading about them is not enough – actually *practicing* them is your key to long-term success!

6. THE POWER OF LANGUAGE

Positive phrasing: Taking advantage of the power of language

Many negotiators think that having good arguments is enough to convince others. There are, indeed, negotiators who manage to come out on top by using loud, blustering, and demonstrative behavior – but they are frequently left wondering why the results that they pushed through are not actually implemented. When they ask the other party, the answer is often something to the effect of: "We felt like we were being cajoled, but not actually convinced." In this chapter, we are going to deal with the power of language. You will learn about the role that your words play in bringing about favorable negotiation outcomes on your behalf.

The eight rules of skilled argumentation

This chapter owes much of its content to Dr. Dieter Portner's 2000 book "Überzeugend diskutieren" ("Persuasive Argumentation"). In his book, Portner compiles field-tested guidelines that teach readers how to use important techniques of argumentation, how to employ language strategically, and how to utilize the power of persuasion to deliver targeted knockout arguments. Since it is hardly possible to negotiate without debating back and forth, you will find the top eight rules for skilled argumentation below – but first, the following self-assessment and case study will illustrate them for you.

SELF-ASSESSMENT 6.1

Nellie wants to get married. Neil does not. Nellie has good arguments in her favor. Neil does too.

Nellie loves Neil. She wants to be with him forever. She wants to have children. She doesn't want to have to pay inheritance taxes on their joint apartment should something happen to Neil.

Neil also wants children... but not yet. He loves Nellie – and he doesn't need a marriage certificate to prove it. He says, "I'm young. Nothing's going to happen to me." And, "It's just a piece of paper – and most marriages end in divorce anyway nowadays."

For the last two hours, they have been sitting at the kitchen table, where they always sit when they have something to negotiate between themselves. The mood is tense. Nellie is growing testier, while Neil is getting brusquer. The pauses in their conversation are growing longer.

NELLIE: You're using such cheap, worn-out arguments.

NEIL: You're obviously just trying to change the topic because you're completely confused.

NELLIE: Great, thanks for showing me just how useless I am.

NEIL: You sound like you're trying to be funny, but without a sense of humor. And I'm supposed to marry someone like that?

NELLIE: You can't come up with any good arguments, so you deliberately twist the facts. It's not the first time.

NEIL: There's just one thing I want to know: Do you actually believe the things you're saying?

For each attack, think of a counter-argument that could help bring Nellie and Neil back to having a constructive dialogue. You can find the solution at the end of the chapter.

CASE STUDY: AT A LOSS FOR WORDS (1)

Neil accompanies his boss, Dr. Valentin Schuster, to an open community forum regarding the new runway that the aerospace company is planning to build for testing prototypes on its newly expanded premises. As an expert from the company, Dr. Schuster is at today's event to answer any initial questions from local citizens. Things get off to a good start. Dr. Schuster has lots of factual information. He brings forth his arguments and observations in a precise, disciplined, and matter-of-fact manner. His voice is steady and unwavering. He articulates his words clearly. He sits up straight; his movements are highly economical. He avoids personal remarks, jokes, and metaphors. He has prepared a comprehensive PowerPoint presentation and makes recourse to plenty of facts and figures.

Suddenly, an extremely committed local activist speaks up. "Dr. Schuster, do you think it's right that millions are being wasted on the defense industry while we're in a financial crisis? I mean, you're damaging the environment to produce spurious products – while at the same time, our schools don't have the money they need to hire enough teachers. Your son is in the same fifth-grade class as my daughter – you know what the situation is like!"

"I..." Dr. Schuster is at a loss for words. A TV camera is fixed on him; the reporter can't help but grin. The scene will be broadcast on the local news that evening. On the drive back to the office, Dr. Schuster opens up to Neil. "I thought I had chosen my arguments so carefully. But I think I need to prepare my presentation even more thoroughly next time around. I only came up with a good response to that woman now." Neil is not so sure that the problem was faulty preparation. In spontaneous situations, Dr. Schuster often found himself at a loss for words. Being better prepared would only lead to him going into even more detail – and simply boring everyone in the room. Why is Dr. Schuster getting stuck? What advice can Neil give his boss?

▶ ANSWER

The eight rules of skilled argumentation from this chapter can help Dr. Schuster.

1. Prepare your arguments thoroughly and determine your own personal negotiation goal.

- Collect as many arguments as possible, both for and against. List them in order of importance. Focus your argumentation on a few strong ("high-powered") arguments, while avoiding weak ("low-powered") arguments or stumbling blocks that could actually undermine your own position.
- Familiarize yourself with a variety of debate techniques, so that you are well-equipped even when you need to respond spontaneously.
- Get written documents that substantiate your arguments. It's best to commit a few bullet points to memory, in order to avoid the risk of having to read off the documents, thus interrupting your direct contact with your counterpart.
- Find out all about your counterpart. You can even write yourself some notes to bring along to the negotiation.

2. Take advantage of the power of first impressions.

- Be friendly – it builds both affinity and trust. Make sure to take some time for small talk. Show up on time – and be positive and engaged right from the start. Be persuasive not only on a substantive level, but also on a human level.
- Refrain from being ostentatious, but don't be too casual or relaxed either.
- Ask your counterpart something about himself right away – don't just talk about yourself.
- Address your counterpart by name.

3. Argue as enthusiastically as possible

- If what you want to "ignite" within your counterpart is something that "burns" inside you, then there is a good chance that you will be successful.
- With commitment, energy, and drive, you can easily compensate for other weaknesses. And if you are the quiet type: come out of your skin – take action and initiative! Try it. It works.

4. Argue descriptively and impressively

- Adapt your arguments to your counterpart.
- Use vivid statements and comparisons.
- Bring in persuasive examples, quotes, anecdotes, etc. "We didn't get the last Chinese contract and it cost us $20 millions. We need to send the team for cultural training so that they're ready for our next negotiations this summer – it's a matter of $30 millions."
- Speak to emotions; "emotionalize" things. "We're concerned about your decision!"
- Stress common ground. "We're both experienced with the Chinese market."
- Use illustrative materials (when possible). "This study by the Max Planck Institute shows that..."
- Be concise. A long list of examples is usually not as powerful as a single inherently strong argument.
- If you will present several arguments, then present your strongest argument last – and your second-strongest argument first. (This method was pioneered by former German Foreign Minister Hans-Dietrich Genscher.)

5. Pay attention to substantive content and logical relationships.

- Stay on topic.
- Don't cram all of your arguments into your opening statement. Leave yourself something in reserve in case you need it later on – have an ace in the hole, an arrow in the quiver.
- Take advantage of the "serial position effect". First impressions (the "primacy effect") and last impressions (the "recency effect") are especially decisive.
- Argue in a logical and structured manner.

6. Be quick-witted and flexible.

- Try to react without that "moment of shock".
- Have a stock of potent answers at the ready.
- Demonstrate mental agility – you should be able to express reactions ranging from deliberate firmness to casual adaptability to full acquiescence.

7. Demonstrate that you are capable of listening.

- Good negotiators are open to the opinions and viewpoints of others while negotiating.
- Use "active listening" techniques.

8. Stay upbeat and relaxed.

- A relaxed demeanor is always good – tense negotiators are usually the ones who hold poor cards. *"Be more relaxed than an excitable person, but more engaged than a disinterested person."* (Rupert Lay)
- Do not allow yourself to be provoked. Being highly combative or aggressive rarely pays off.
- Your negotiation counterpart may be your "opponent" – but you should never see him as your "enemy".

Wording Tips

Keep things personal by using personal pronouns (e.g., I, we, you).

Although common in everyday speech, avoid using the unnecessarily weak-sounding "polite conditional" when negotiating – i.e., instead of "I would suggest...", state simply "I suggest..." You need to leave a strong impression when you are trying to persuade someone!

Instead of "The problem is...", say "Here's the situation..." We often throw around the word "problem" for things that are not truly problems – just situations or issues that need to be cleared up. Only use the word "problem" when something really is a genuine problem.

Avoid using wishy-washy words and phrases like "I think...", "I believe...", "I would say...", "Perhaps..." Instead, pause briefly at strategic moments, taking advantage of the power of silence. These "power pauses" allow your counterpart a bit of time to wrap his mind around what you have said.

Constructing an argument

Good substantive content is obviously quite persuasive. But when both sides have compelling substantive arguments, the party that structures his argument more skillfully will prevail.

The "Persuasive Selling Format"

Below you will learn a structure that has been proven successful millions of times. You can use it whenever you need to persuade someone of something in a negotiation. You can also use it as a basic structure for a PowerPoint presentation that you may use to push some specific proposal or option during the course of your negotiations. Or you can follow the five steps in a dialogue with your counterpart, using questions to take him through the steps one by one.

The "Persuasive Selling Format" trains negotiators to be disciplined and makes sure that no questions – whether substantive or psychological – remain unanswered.

The five steps will be described in detail below.

1. Summarize the situation
- Describe the status quo

QUESTIONS TO BE ANSWERED:
- What exactly do we want to change?
- What is not working?
- What are we missing and why?
- What can be improved?

GOAL:
- Counterpart starts getting interested in the matter

2. State your idea
- Mention your solution
- Outline options

QUESTIONS TO BE ANSWERED:
- What exactly is my idea?
- What benefits does it offer?
- What options do we have?

GOAL:
- Counterpart understands the proposal
- Argument is coherent and consistent

3. Explain how it works
- Demonstrate the idea's feasibility
- Describe the various options in detail
- Anticipate questions and objections

QUESTIONS TO BE ANSWERED:
- Who should do what? By when? How?

GOAL:
- Generate an understanding of the process
- Prove the idea's feasibility

4. Reinforce key benefits
- Substantiate idea/proposal
- Repeat key arguments
- Spell out explicitly benefits/advantages to your counterpart

QUESTIONS TO BE ANSWERED:
- How do you benefit from our proposal?
- How do we benefit from our proposal?

GOAL:
- Make it easy for them to go along

5. Suggest easy next steps
- Identify first concrete actions to be taken
- Define timing/responsibilities

QUESTIONS TO BE ANSWERED:
- Who will do what? By when? How?
- Is a test run possible?

GOAL:
- Make the decision easy
- Plan implementation

CASE STUDY: NEIL NEEDS HELP

Neil wants to convince his boss to hire a temporary employee for six months to help out on a new order. He knows that Dr. Schuster is as strict with the department budget as he is with his own personal finances. Neil's coworkers tell him that there's no chance the boss will accept his suggestion – "Many have tried, none have succeeded," they say. To prepare for his negotiation, Neil makes use of the "Persuasive Selling Format". Here is what his argument looks like:

1. The new client from the U.A.E. is very important to the future of our company. They're planning additional major projects. They want to equip their police with our helicopters. Future cooperation will depend upon the efficiency and quality with which we carry out this first order. At the moment, I am so swamped with other ongoing projects that I don't have the time necessary to dedicate to this one.

2. My idea is to bring in Martin Mohrmann to help out on this project. He's a SAP expert. He helped us out on that big contract we got from Brazil on short notice last year – he does great work and he's free at the moment.

3. I can bring him into the loop myself. We've been working for years with the agency he goes through, and it's always worked out well for us. We bring Martin in for six months, and then later we can decide if we want to hire him long term or just let his contract expire.

4. I will be able to start dedicating my efforts fully to leading the new project right away. Strategically, this project is very important to us – the CEO himself recently spoke about the potential benefits of having the U.A.E. as a major client. And there's really no risk in taking Martin on for six months – we can choose afterwards if we want to keep him here.

5. I can arrange an interview with Martin for next week, so that you can get to know him. What do you think of my proposal?

ONEPAGER – How to prepare your arguments for a negotiation

1. Summarize the situation
- What exactly is the problem?
- Whose problem is it?
- What does the status quo look like for each party?
- How can you interest the other side in your issue?

2. State your idea
- What exactly do you want to change?
- What do you hope to achieve?
- What is your idea or objective?
- What can you do to change the baseline situation?

3. Explain how it works
- What background information do you want to give?
- What details can underscore your expertise in the matter?
- What information will help keep things transparent?
- What questions or objections can you anticipate?

4. Reinforce key benefits
- What does the other side get out of it?
- How will you explicitly address these benefits?

5. Suggest easy next steps
- What now?
- Where can we go from here?
- How can the proposal be concretized?
- Is there an action plan? Who must do what? By when?

Want to lead? Learn how to ask questions like a seasoned pro

In the context of negotiations, questioning techniques represent a communication tool that is often undervalued – and thus not utilized as purposefully as it should be. There are three essential types of questions: open-ended questions, multiple-choice questions, and closed-ended questions. You can take control of your negotiations by using these three question types properly. You will mostly work with open-ended questions as you try to get information from the other party during the opening and exploratory phases at the start of the negotiations, as well as while developing options. At later stages of the negotiations, such as while evaluating the available options, you can use multiple-choice questions. And towards the end of the negotiation process, when it's all about reaching a final agreement, closed-ended questions are helpful.

In the following chart, you will find information regarding these and several other types of questions, as well as the goals that can be achieved with each.

Type of question	Goal	Examples
Open-ended questions	• Getting information • Open-ended questions advance the discussion by bringing out both qualitative information and the other parties' opinions.	The five W's (and one H): • Who? • What? • When? • Where? • Why? • How?
Closed-ended questions	• Reaching decisions	Can only be answered with "yes" or "no": • Can we agree upon this? • Do you want to order the goods?

Multiple-choice questions	• Choosing between options	Require a choice between two or more alternatives: • Would it be easier for you to accommodate us on the quality or the timing?
Leading questions	• Consciously trying to influence the other party	Deftly lead the other party to a particular answer: • Surely you see things the same way? • So you would agree that...? • And have you noticed as well that...?
Counterquestions	• Dodging another question • Getting some time to think things over • Learning about the other party's objections	• But what exactly do you mean when you say that our proposal is not fair?
Motivational questions	• Cultivating the relationship with compliments	• How did you complete that project so quickly?
Provocative questions	• Breaking through the other party's reserve	• Are you really willing to pass up these huge benefits?
Echo questions	• Showing empathy and understanding	• We're already on agreement on most points, right?

TIP:

Ask as many solution-oriented questions as possible: "What has to happen for...?" "What would be an ideal outcome for you?" "Can you help me understand what exactly you are seeking?" "What can we do to ease your concerns?"

And ask follow-up questions, especially question that help concretize matters: "So you're willing to work with us on the price? Exactly how much of a discount can you offer us?" "You can deliver fast? By when would we need to provide you the exact quantity of units for the order?"

Quick responsiveness in negotiations

A sharp-tongued question, a moody opponent, or a malicious attack – these are some of the classic situations in which you need to be quick on the comeback. One of your goals in a negotiation is to retain the upper hand, so you cannot let yourself get defeated in a war of words. You need to be self-confident and meet your counterpart at eye level.

But when you're caught off-guard in uncomfortable situations, you can end up at a loss for words – or even start babbling helplessly against something. Instead of you controlling the situation, the situation controls you. But one can actually learn how to be ready with a response. Below you will discover five techniques that will help you respond to others quickly and confidently.

CASE STUDY: AT A LOSS FOR WORDS (2)

Dr. Schuster's own manager has seen the uncomfortable video clip on the evening news. The next morning, he calls Dr. Schuster into his office for a talk. They decide that Dr. Schuster will undergo coaching to help him better deliver his arguments. His first appointment is just a few days later.

The coach introduces Dr. Schuster to five ways to avoid getting stuck in the same predicament in the future:

1. Silence
2. The translation technique
3. Counterquestions
4. The "that's-exactly-why" technique
5. The evasion technique

Dr. Schuster listens skeptically, thinking: *It sounds simple in theory, but how does it actually work in practice?* After the theoretical lesson, though, he will have to try out the techniques himself.

1. Silence

Silence is a very simple yet highly effective technique. You say nothing at first – instead, simply wait. It is important to maintain eye contact – do not feel sheepish and look away. With your silence, you are challenging your counterpart: "Don't just come at me with personal attacks – that stuff bounces right off me. I'm big enough to not even react." You then control the situation. You decide when to reply. This may not seem like a literal example of being "quick on the comeback" – yet, interestingly enough, it works just the same.

The critical element of the waiting technique is remaining passive. Sometimes you may manage to bring the situation to a close by terminating your eye contact. You will often end up having to counter the other party's attack verbally, in order to avoid being the "victim"; in this sense, waiting in silence is a sort of "bridging" technique.

The silence technique is especially well-suited to the following situations:

- Allowing tantrums to fizzle out
- When you are confronted with blanket accusations
- As a "gentle" way to deal with higher-ranking negotiation counterparts
- When you want to gain valuable seconds to formulate a sharp response

CASE STUDY: AT A LOSS FOR WORDS (3)

The coach challenges Dr. Schuster to respond using the silence technique. "I'm getting the sense you don't have what it takes," she says.

Dr. Schuster tilts his head and raises an eyebrow, without saying a word, while maintaining eye contact with the coach.

"Great," she says, "that's just how it works in practice. First of all, you gain some time. You don't have to deal with the insulting remarks or malicious insinuations. You force your opponent to keep talking – to explain their accusations or give more information. This is usually enough to cool them down a bit. And your silence also helps avoid the escalation that would occur if you were to lash out right back at them."

---

2. The translation technique

The translation technique is very simple yet effective. Essentially, you repeat in different words what the other party has just said. Almost any attack can be dealt with using this flexible technique, so it pays to practice it often enough that it becomes second nature to you. How does it work?

You basically act as an interpreter, translating your opponent's malicious words. For example: "So you mean to say that..." It may not sound very spectacular, but it opens up unforeseen possibilities. You take it upon yourself to explain to your counterpart what he just said – but in your own words. You thus take control of the direction in which the discussion will proceed.

The translation technique is especially well-suited to the following situations:

- Responding to personal insults
- Responding to unintentional slights
- Responding to accusations and baseless criticism

As a quick-witted translator, you will have recourse to three "tongues":

- A "sweet tongue", with which you interpret even the most venomous attacks as pleasant compliments. (Obviously your opponent does not share your positive view of things – but as long as he contradicts you, you have warded off his attack.)

Example: "You're so fussy about your requirements." "So you mean to say that we're extremely precise about everything? That's true – and the fact that we pay such attention to the details means that, after we reach an agreement, there won't be any surprises later on for either one of us."

- A "poisonous tongue", with which you interpret hidden slights as being even more offensive. (Your opponent will respond by rejecting your "poisonous" interpretation and apologizing.) Example: "You're so fussy about your requirements." "So you mean to say we're nothing more than petty bean counters?" "No, no, I didn't mean it quite like that."

- A "diplomatic tongue", with which you smooth out sharp tones and bring yourself into a more advantageous position. (You can use the other side's dissent to make the discussion more objective; prompt your opponent to state what exactly he meant to say.) Example: "You're so fussy about your requirements." "So you think we don't need to settle all of the details now, but rather just set out a general framework? Can you explain how you see our expectations being met then?"

CASE STUDY: AT A LOSS FOR WORDS (4)

Dr. Schuster's training continues. His coach explains that the translation technique is really simple. "With the use of a trigger phrase like 'So you mean...', you can get your own thoughts pointed in the right direction. Then you just follow it up with your 'translation'. Let's try it out. Imagine that we're in a negotiation and I attack you, saying, 'Everything you're claiming is a lie!'"

"So you mean... you'd like to see copies of the studies to which I'm referring?" replies Dr. Schuster immediately. "Exactly," says the coach, "it's as simple as that."

---

3. Counterquestions

The person who asks questions is in control. And the person who does not want to be controlled by others asks right back and takes control himself! Counterquestions are useful, as they allow you to stay in the driver's seat and prevent you from delivering yourself right into your opponent's hands. Follow-up questions are similar to counterquestions – except that these are not in response to a question, but rather in response to an attack by your opponent. Counterquestions and follow-up questions come in many shades – from politely neutralizing to harshly aggressive. And although a counterquestion can trigger tension, it tends to be a mild technique that you can comfortably use in negotiations with your boss or with difficult clients. Skillfully employing counterquestions and follow-up questions can allow you to subtly bring a conversation back to the substantive level.

This technique is especially well-suited to the following situations:

- Responding to provocative, intrusive, or indiscreet questions
- Dealing with tense atmospheres
- Responding to "sledgehammer" attacks
- Responding to insinuations

Some counterquestions are essentially counterattacks. These sorts of counterquestions enter into play when you are in competitive negotiations and want to take a hard stand – you should only use them when your opponent's questions are truly unfair. Here are some examples:

- "Why are you twisting my words?"
- "Why are you asking?" / "Weren't you listening to what I said?"
- "What are you talking about?" / "Where did you get that idea?"

- "Why aren't you trying to understand what I'm saying?"
- "You're not fully informed – why didn't you do your research beforehand?"

These counterquestions have quite a strong effect. Even though supposedly "tough" negotiators love using them as a rhetorical tool, there's a catch – such sentences involve insinuations, which impede a climate of trust. Any third parties will take note and will learn to exercise caution when dealing with you in the future. This is likewise the case if you intimidate your opponent to such an extent that he doesn't even dare to respond.

CASE STUDY: AT A LOSS FOR WORDS (5)

"You're a troublemaker!" the argumentation coach yells at Dr. Schuster.

"What do you mean I'm a troublemaker? Is that your way of saying that I actually have my own opinion? Would you rather just be surrounded by a bunch of yes-men?" Dr. Schuster really gets going.

"Not bad, in principle," says the coach. "But when you ask so many questions like that, one after another, the conversation can start sounding like an interrogation. Your opponents feel like they're being grilled, and this creates an unpleasant atmosphere."

4. The "that's-exactly-why" technique

This next technique is a way to avoid constantly rebutting ("That's not true, because..."), talking down ("It's not quite that bad, because..."), or pushing aside ("Yes, but on the other hand...") your opponent's objections. It enables you to instantly rebut the objection, while still taking it seriously. You express agreement – and then immediately continue by saying "that's exactly why...", to argue in favor of your own idea or offering. This technique shows confidence, but it only works when two conditions are met:

- There is a coherent link between your opponent's objection and the benefits that you will highlight in response.The benefits that you will highlight outweigh your opponent's objection.

CASE STUDY: AT A LOSS FOR WORDS (6)

The coach explains the "that's-exactly-why" technique to Dr. Schuster – and then she asks him to try it out. "Let's say you're trying to sell me a helicopter, and I complain that your price is too high. How would you respond?"

Dr. Schuster pauses for a moment, then replies, "Yes, our helicopters do cost $30 millions – and that's exactly why we can offer you first-rate quality and a 20-year warranty."

"Perfect," says the coach.

5. The evasion technique

The evasion technique involves one negotiator apparently paying attention to the other, listening without interruption – but when his counterpart is finished talking, he replies with a change of topic. Negotiators who have lots of power or influence like to use this technique; the other party rarely objects or complains. But it's best not to actually use this technique – rather simply be aware of it, so that you can counter it in the event that your opponent uses it. Point out his evasiveness and insist on returning to the topic at hand – being hard on the issues, but soft towards the person, of course.

CASE STUDY: AT A LOSS FOR WORDS (7)

Dr. Schuster has the following dialogue with his coach:

COACH: Dr. Schuster, your proposal has clearly been very well thought out. But instead of discussing it today, we should rather talk about whether...

DR. SCHUSTER: Let's return to the proposal – it's what's on the agenda for today.

COACH: Well, the reasoning behind your plan is quite convincing. But first, let's consider another aspect...

DR. SCHUSTER: Before we consider this new aspect, I'd like to add that...

The dialectics of war and peace

The word "dialectic" comes from the Greek *dialegein* ("to converse"). Dialectic is the art of discourse – the ability to arrive at a higher truth via the discussion and comparison of conflicting propositions. This is something essential to negotiation.

According to renowned German rhetoric coach Rupert Lay, the art of dialectic (*ars dialectica*) can be divided into two domains: the dialectic of peace and the dialectic of war. In the context of negotiations, competitive negotiators will generally prefer the dialectic of war, while cooperative negotiators will tend towards the dialectic of peace.

The goals of the dialectic of peace are consensus, compromise, and joint problem-solving. Everything must be done fairly – a fair discussion is most important to all negotiating parties. Efforts are made to deal with each other in a cooperative manner. If no agreement or solution is achieved, then the parties remain in peaceful coexistence, on equal footing, each with their own different points of view. And they can sit down at the negotiating table together again in the future. Their attitude is basically: "We didn't reach a consensus this time – but maybe next time!"

In the dialectic of war, it's all about pushing through one's own position and objectives at any cost – and thus defeating one's opponent. Almost anything goes – even unfair attacks and aggressive countermeasures. Strategic toughness and tactical chicanery are used to verbally "beat up" one's opponent.

There are classic rhetorical techniques behind both these forms of dialectic, and you will become familiar with them below; without a doubt, you have already encountered some of them in discussions you have held in your own life. In the case of the dialectic of war, you will particularly learn how to fend off such rhetorical attacks – and ideally redirect the rhetoric towards a return to the dialectic of peace.

The seven classic techniques of the dialectic of war

At some point, you may have experienced the following situation: You bring out good arguments in the negotiating room, trying to understand the other side's arguments as well – but then suddenly the tone of the conversation changes. The atmosphere goes cold. Your position is under attack, and nothing makes sense anymore. You had thought you were on the right path, but now suddenly you're left speechless – in shock, anger, or confusion. You desperately try to defend yourself with different arguments, but it seems like there's no way out. The other side is superior to you rhetorically and has pushed you into a corner.

If you familiarize yourself with the seven classic techniques of the dialectic of war, it will be easier for you to keep the "helicopter perspective" and react accordingly.

The dialectic of war: Ad personam attacks

Instead of making substantive arguments, the other party may attack, denigrate, or insult you on a personal level.

EXAMPLES:

- "It's people like you who make life difficult for us."
- "You don't seem up to the task of negotiating with high-level managers."
- "It's just impossible to work with you."
- "There's nothing more unbearable than a modern career woman."

YOUR DEFENSE:

Stay calm. Absolutely do *not* strike back in the same manner. In your response, you can lay bare just how unfairly your opponent is acting. *"Insults are the arguments employed by those who are in the wrong."* (Rousseau)

The dialectic of war: The series of "yeses"

The other party may deftly use a series of questions that can be answered with a "yes", in order to get you to instinctively answer yes to his last question as well.

EXAMPLE:

- "Is your company involved with the local community?" ("Yes.")
- "Then I'm sure you must have strong environmental compliance policies in place, right?" ("Yes.")
- "So can I introduce you to our wonderful training course, entitled 'The Environmentally Conscious Employee'?" ("Yes.")

YOUR DEFENSE:

Stay alert so that you can recognize when a counterpart is planning to use this tactic (keywords include: certainly, definitely, I'm sure). A single "no" will break the chain.

The dialectic of war: Flattery

Here, the other party deliberately flatters you, in order to induce you to make concessions – often much sooner than you should.

EXAMPLES:

- "You're really an expert in this area. With your professional qualifications, I'm sure you'll agree that it would be impossible for us to guarantee quality at that price."
- "With your extensive international experience, I presume you understand that we need to meet our deadline with the Chinese."

YOUR DEFENSE:

Accept the compliment and politely thank your counterpart for it – but separate it from the substantive question of concessions.

The dialectic of war: Showing off

By using lots of buzzwords, the other party tries to give the impression that they have a high level of expertise.

EXAMPLE:

- "Profit-oriented customer service management is focused on estimated future value, i.e., potential earning capacity from the customer relationship, taking into account the targeted and systematic configuration of the customer-specific relationship and dialogue processes based on the level of target customer satisfaction, which in turn is distilled from insights yielded by customer service satisfaction analyses."

YOUR DEFENSE:

Insist upon a translation into common speech. "As a professional, I'm sure you can get your point across in a more comprehensible manner."

The dialectic of war: Relativization

Anything can be relativized by saying that "it depends..." This is always a true statement. A negotiator may try to use such statements to generalize something concrete, or vice versa.

EXAMPLES:

- "Your example is an isolated case and has to be looked at accordingly."
- "You're right about that particular situation, but those sorts of things depend on the circumstances."
- "That varies from case to case."
- "You need to look at this differently."

YOUR DEFENSE:

Expose your opponent's use of the relativization technique, speaking to its generality – and return to the point you were trying to make.

The dialectic of war: Attacking vulnerabilities

An opposing party may focus on a single inaccurate, exaggerated, or generally weak argument of yours (a "low-power" or "no-power" argument), refuting it resoundingly and demonstratively, in order to devalue and undermine your overall presentation.

EXAMPLES:

- "Your claim that... has been proven wrong – this means your whole position is wrong."
- "You're not up to date on the latest technology. The most recent study proves... Maybe you should go do some homework before we even discuss any of this further."

YOUR DEFENSE:

Accept the correction, then redirect the conversation back to your strongest arguments. Say simply, "That was a slight oversight", or "Thanks for the tip, I'll look into this", or "Yes, you're right in that regard, but keep in mind the much stronger argument in favor of our proposal, which is that..."

The dialectic of war: Exaggeration

The other party may deliberately exaggerate individual points, or even your entire position, to the point where they seem irrational, absurd, or dangerous.

EXAMPLES:

- "You've never met me halfway."
- "You always try to get an ever bigger discount right when we're reaching the end of the negotiations."
- "Just the slightest bit of intelligence is all that's needed to solve this problem."

YOUR DEFENSE:

Say it like it is – address the exaggeration directly and ask for substantive arguments instead: "You're seriously exaggerating. Can you please clarify again what you see as the root problem here?"

The seven classic techniques of the dialectic of peace

You might also have experienced a situation where, despite wanting to cooperate, you realize that you are getting easily provoked – so you frantically search for words to de-escalate the situation. Below, you will get to know seven classic rhetorical techniques for cooperation.

The dialectic of peace: Demonstrating

Your argument is substantiated and reinforced by a vivid example, metaphor, comparison, or object (photo, magazine, sketch, graphic, etc.) This is an especially effective technique, because images are understood easily and remembered longer – your counterpart will keep a "mental picture" of what you have said.

EXAMPLES:

- "We're all pulling in the same direction."
- "We're all in the same boat here."
- "We're living in stormy times, and it's not always so easy to find a port in the storm."

TRIGGER PHRASES

- "Imagine..."
- "Have you ever experienced...?"
- "Do you know what happened to me recently? ..."
- "Aren't you aware of the case...?"

The dialectic of peace: Disarming

You can take the wind out of your opponent's sails by acknowledging yourself his (patently accurate) criticism, complaint, or argument. This technique has been used since ancient times. In practice, your unexpected agreement with your counterpart's line of argument, or your admission of your own shortcomings, will – with surprising frequency – shock them. Sometimes you will leave them so stunned that they will literally be speechless – it doesn't make sense for an attacker any longer to keep attacking you if you are agreeing with him!

EXAMPLES:

- "Thank you for your critical comments – I understand your complaint."
- "It's a good thing you brought this to our attention – we'll have to work on improving it."
- "You're right – our mistake. What can we do to make sure it doesn't happen again?"

The dialectic of peace: Compromising

In cases where strong differences of opinion, discords, rivalries, or intransigent positions are at play, often the only solution is to compromise – i.e., both sides meet in the middle. Rigid stances mean the end of the discussion – results can only be achieved by the parties mutually moving towards each other.

EXAMPLES:

- "We won't get anywhere if we continue like this – each of us has got to make some concessions."
- "We can meet you halfway on that point – on which point can you meet us halfway?"
- "Our points of view are quite clear now – so where can we find common ground?

The dialectic of peace: Repetition

Constant dripping wears away a stone – so keep at it! Don't give up after your first try. Repeating compelling points several times in an unobtrusive manner significantly strengthens their effect. *"There is only one figure in rhetoric of serious importance – repetition."* (Napoleon). When we hear something for the first time, it's still foreign to us – but when we hear it again and again, it's already familiar to us.

EXAMPLES:

- "Let me explain again, in other words, why this is so important."
- "Like I said earlier – we need to change our market strategy if we want to get into this market."
- "And I repeat, emphatically..."

The dialectic of peace: The "we-feeling"

Appeal to social responsibility and a sense of community in order to advance your own objectives. Leverage the power of a need for solidarity and common ground.

EXAMPLES:

- "You also want to reach a solution that you can sell internally, right?"
- "Haven't we always found solutions? Let's make sure we stick together this time too."
- "I know how you feel. I used to be in the same situation too, so I can really put myself in your shoes."

The dialectic of peace: Academic or scientific sources

Citing academic or scientific studies or well-reputed experts strengthens one's arguments and claims. Such recourses also give the impression of high professional competency – which immediately boosts your credibility. A distinction should be made here between reputable, factual sources and dubious research based on incorrect "facts" and unverified claims. Listen critically, and challenge your counterpart's sources if necessary.

EXAMPLES:

- "After consulting with our finance team, we can..."
- "All the IT experts are in agreement that..."
- "Dr. Schubert from Stanford is a leading figure in this field, and he concluded from his research that..."
- "According to a Smithsonian study from last year..."

The dialectic of peace: Diagnostic argumentation

Diagnostic argumentation looks at three things: Situation – Objective – Measures. This framework is extremely versatile and highly transparent. You can get agreements from your counterpart relatively easily, as long as your description of the situation sticks to the facts – and not to false facts! ☺ – and your description of the objective includes your counterpart's own objectives. A common foundation is created, on the basis of which the negotiation can determine the best measures to take.

EXAMPLE:

- "The tax laws are constantly changing. Our tax department is understaffed, and we're giving away millions. So we need to hire a new member to join our team."

SOLUTION TO SELF-ASSESSMENT 6.1

NELLIE: You're using such cheap, worn-out arguments.

Possible reply by NEIL: Nellie, that just shows that even though you've heard my arguments many times before, you still don't entirely understand exactly what I'm trying to say.

→ With his response, Neil takes Nellie's attack and brings it around to the question of her substantive understanding.

NEIL: You're obviously just trying to change the topic because you're completely confused.

Possible reply by NELLIE: I'm sorry if that's the impression you get. I'd be glad to explain again more clearly exactly why it is that I want to get married now.

> → Nellie apologizes for how she has expressed herself, but sticks to her points instead of reacting to the attack.

NELLIE: Great, thanks for showing me just how useless I am.

Possible reply by NEIL: (holding eye contact and pausing, then smiling) Honey, now you finally understand why I love you so much. (pause) Come on, let's talk seriously again about how we see the situation here.

> → Instead of reacting seriously to the attack, Neil replies ironically. His smile and his second sentence signal to Nellie his affection and respect.

NEIL: You sound like you're trying to be funny, but without a sense of humor. And I'm supposed to marry someone like that?

Possible reply by NELLIE: I don't think we're getting anywhere with this right now – let's sleep on it and discuss things tomorrow, okay?

> → Instead of reacting to the insult, Nellie recognizes that she and Neil are stuck in a stalemate. She actively suggests adjourning the discussion until the following day. She also gets Neil to agree with her on this.

NELLIE: You can't come up with any good arguments, so you deliberately twist the facts. It's not the first time.

Possible reply by NEIL: Nellie, be careful what you say. You place so much value on us being able to talk openly and honestly with each other. Don't start insinuating that I twist the facts just because you're frustrated.

→ Neil does not give in to the attack, objecting to it clearly by making reference to the "standards" that are important to Nellie in their relationship.

NEIL: There's just one thing I want to know: Do you actually believe the things you're saying?

Possible reply by NELLIE: So what do you think is important to me? I want you to try to tell me in your own words – how do you understand the things I've said?

→ Nellie makes use of counterquestions. Instead of replying directly to the attack, she thus brings it back around to Neil and to the actual substance of the discussion.

SUMMARY: THE POWER OF LANGUAGE

▶ **What are the best rules for skilled argumentation?**

- Argue vividly and impressively.
- Use rhetorical devices such as metaphors, storytelling, analogies, and other comparisons.
- Be an active listener. Follow up with questions if necessary.
- Avoid wishy-washy language – instead, use power pauses and rhetorical intensifiers.

▶ **How to structure your argumentation in line with the "Persuasive Selling Format":**

- Summarize the situation.
- State your idea.
- Explain how it works.
- Reinforce key benefits.
- Suggest easy next steps.

▶ **How to make well-directed use of questioning techniques:**

- Ask open-ended questions at the initial stages of a negotiation in order to get information.
- Ask closed-ended questions at the later stages in order to reach a result.

▶ **How to quickly overcome unpleasant situations in a negotiation**

- Using silence, you can show your strength.
- Using the "translation" technique, you can bring the other party back to the substantive level.

- Using counterquestions, you can dig deeper and clarify matters.
- Using the "that's-exactly-why" technique, you can keep the upper hand.
- Using the evasion technique, you can gain time.

▶ **How to use the dialectics of peace or war in a negotiation:**

- The seven classic techniques of the dialectic of war are ways to force your own position through.
- The seven classic techniques of the dialectic of peace are ways to help a negotiation move towards a consensus.

7. BODY LANGUAGE AND INTUITION

Natural tools – Facial expressions, gestures, and posture

According to a frequently cited study carried out by psychology professor Albert Mehrabian in the seventies, the majority of a person's communication is conveyed via body language. When Mehrabian asked his students how they thought people got their messages across, the students made reference to the contents of the message, the arguments in its favor, etc.

Mehrabian had hired two actors and told them that he would introduce them to the class as experts who would each give lectures on the same topic – but the two lectures would be quite different. One lecturer would be extremely well-versed in the topic, with a profound understanding of its finer details – but his presentation would be undermined by an absentminded demeanor, a monotonous delivery, and a lack of eye contact. The other actor's lecture would be exactly the opposite: His knowledge of the subject matter would be extremely thin, such that anyone who listened closely would notice slight mistakes and inconsistencies – yet he would deliver his lecture in an enthusiastic and vibrant manner, keeping the students engaged.

After the two actors had delivered their lectures to the class, Professor Mehrabian asked his students which of the two had been more credible and convincing. The charismatic lecturer won out by a large margin. From a more detailed analysis of his experiments, Professor Mehrabian came to the surprising conclusion that about 7% of the effects of our speech can be attributed to our words (i.e., their content), about 38% to our voice, and about 55% to our body language.

What does this mean in the context of negotiation?

- Your words (i.e., content) should be clear.

- Your voice should be strong.
- Your body language and other nonverbal communication should be confident.

What you want to achieve is not the only thing that matters – *how* you express yourself is at least as important. Your body language and voice play crucial roles in this regard. Your body language and voice are "natural tools" that are always available to you in your personal communication repository. If a carpenter were to use his tools incorrectly, then it would be difficult for him to produce a good piece of furniture; likewise, if you employ your body language incorrectly, then it will be difficult for you to reach a good negotiation result – no matter how strong your arguments may be.

There must be consistency between what you expect from a negotiation and how you express this with your body and voice – otherwise, your counterpart will not buy into it. If there is a disconnect, your counterpart will always trust what your body language is telling him – it is more powerful than the words that you speak.

SELF-ASSESSMENT 7.1

Nellie's brother Noah wants to start his own business. He is very excited today – he has an appointment with a loan officer from his bank to discuss a start-up loan. For this meeting, he has traded in his usual sweatshirt for a jacket and tie, though he has decided to stick with jeans. He's not trying to win a modeling contest – he simply has a great idea and he's here to talk about money.

LOAN OFFICER: Mr. Nelson, tell me why you need $20,000.

NOAH: *(scratches his head, blushes, smiles crookedly, and mumbles insecurely)* Well, so, everyone knows that you have to run your business like a professional if you want to make it these days, right? *(speeds up)* So basically, what I'm saying is, I need a website, because nothing's possible without an online presence these days, and I've got a good friend who's a programmer – he's definitely going to help me out with that. I asked him recently, he said he could do it. And for the logo and whatnot, obviously I'm going to need to hire someone – I'm going to do some research and find someone who can do it. And I'm going to need a new laptop – I've got to be able to show clients what I can do, right? And the professional software, it costs a fortune. And since I'm trying to start a business as a design engineer, obviously I'm also going to need the latest CAD programs. *(looks at the table and fiddles with his fingers, then realizes that he's fidgeting and presses his hands firmly against his thighs)*

BANKER: I see. So basically you want a loan for the purchase of business equipment and technological services for your new company?

NOAH: *(nods energetically several times, in rapid succession)* Man, it's hot in here – do you have some water? Mineral water if possible, please – tap water doesn't always agree with me.

BANKER: *(passing him a small bottle of water)* Sure. Now, can you explain your business plan a bit more clearly? Who are your clients?

NOAH: So, what I was thinking about was the automotive industry. Maybe also aerospace – my sister's boyfriend makes helicopters. And my senior thesis went over really well. It's definitely got potential, and there's nothing like it yet. *(grabs some loose papers from his bag to show the banker, who waves them off)*

If Noah were to actually get a loan after this conversation, it would be a huge miracle. What can he do better next time? Read the expert opinion at the end of the chapter.

The secret language of negotiation: What your body is saying

Posture, gestures, facial expressions, and eye contact are considered to be the most important ways one expresses oneself while negotiating. Just like a single word has meaning, yet does not represent an entire sentence – so too each individual body part has its own forms of expression, yet only the totality of one's nonverbal expression represents the complete message. In order to understand a language, one needs to learn natural tools – and each individual body part and its various forms of expression constitute the "vocabulary" of one's body language. And just like a language's grammar connects individual words in a meaningful way – so too must one's body language come out "fluently", so as not to appear inconsistent.

From head to toe – The nine most important natural tools of our body language

There is plenty of literature on the topic of body language. One of the top body-language experts in the world is Samy Molcho. He has dealt with body language throughout his entire life, first as a professional mime and later as an author and coach. Many of the tips below are based on his extensive knowledge of the subject.

SAMY MOLCHO

Samy Molcho was born in Israel in 1936 and was on the stage from the age of ten. In addition to the techniques of mime, he studied classical, modern, and far-eastern dance, as well as acting, directing, and drama. He went on to become one of the most important mimes of the 20th century, and is now based in Austria.

Samy Molcho added purely psychological and dramatic elements to the art of mime. His books on the topic of body language, which have been translated into twelve languages, gained him worldwide fame as an author. In his books, he describes the effects of gestures and facial expressions on interpersonal communication.

When you negotiate, you want to make an impact on your counterpart – the worst thing that can happen to you as a negotiator is to be unable to influence the other party. The following nine "natural tools" of negotiation body language will help you take conscious control over your own influence in the future, and also be able to better read the messages that your counterpart is sending.

Natural tool #1: The face

At the start of a negotiation, our counterpart's facial expression is always the first thing we notice. In most cases, we perceive the person's facial expression as a whole, rather than noticing any one particular detail. Our bodies have always followed the lead of our heads – our movements are controlled by our minds. Human beings have more than 650 muscles, and more than 50 of these are located in the face. Smiling requires the use of 17 muscles; frowning requires 40. So what basic signals do our facial expressions send?

When the movement of one's facial muscles is generally upward, as when smiling, then this has a positive effect – whereas a general downward movement makes one surmise fatigue, tension, or other such problems. A negotiator who wants to deceive another will primarily make use of his facial expressions. But we often can quickly detect a put-on smile, fake cheerfulness, or a calculated poker face – we can easily notice that it contradicts what the rest of the person's body language is saying. We sense that the person is "faking it" – and their credibility suffers as a result.

Natural tool #2: The eyes

Even the best argument in the world will be ineffective if it is delivered without making eye contact. You want to know if your counterpart really means what he is saying – so look at him while you are negotiating! Is he holding your gaze? Do his eyes radiate confidence? Is his gaze piercing and dominant? In any case, maintaining eye contact will tell you a lot about your counterpart. Here are some suggestions to help you to leave a positive impression yourself:

Maintain eye contact for at least one second
Anything less than this will not even feel like eye contact. A suggestion for less-experienced negotiators: Choose one or two people in the room who are friendly towards you and look at them more often.

Make firm eye contact while making demands
This makes you seem determined and lends extra weight to what you are requesting. Do not look down when you make demands, nor when you reject the other party's demands.

Avoid cold, calculated stares
Don't forget – hard on the issues, but soft towards the person. Making warm eye contact builds a bridge between you and your counterpart.

If you fix your gaze on him coldly, you will inevitably make him feel uncomfortable with you – and that's not how one builds trust.

Dull glances don't stimulate anyone
Even the best arguments are useless if your eyes show no signs of life.

Make eye contact with everyone in the room
Don't only look at the other party's decision-maker – rather, make eye contact with every single one of his team members. And include members of your own team as well.

Start and end your negotiation by pausing and making eye contact
Cast a confident glance around the room at the start of the negotiation, before you say even a single word. This will give yourself and the other party an opportunity to get focused. Your gaze should then get stronger over the course of the negotiation. And even after you have clearly spoken your final word, cast one final brief glance at your counterpart.

What does it actually mean when you look the other party in the eye? Looking someone in the eye compels them to speak up. People often try to escape this compulsion by blinking, by "looking inwards" (without noticing the other person), or by shifting their gaze to the side. Just this look away is often enough to dissolve the confrontation. In future negotiations, when your counterpart looks away, it's likely because he does not want to be forced into taking a stand or making a decision. You can consciously make matters easier for him by shifting your own gaze first, so that he feels more relaxed and has more time to think over his decision.

How do negotiators express themselves with their eyebrows? Raised eyebrows are a sign of paying attention – the negotiator is trying to increase his field of vision and take in as much information as possible. A single raised eyebrow, on the other hand, expresses skepticism.

Why do some negotiators repeatedly clutch at their glasses? A person who has discovered weaknesses in his own position feels like he needs to take a closer look. Sometimes this is also an expression of worry that some detail has been forgotten. Surprisingly, negotiators who are insecure often clutch at their earlobes – which, in the field of acupuncture, are considered stimulation points for better vision.

Natural tool #3: The nose and mouth

It is through the mouth that we take in what our bodies need. Our mouths also instantly reveal our state of mind, reflecting positive feelings when they curve upwards and negative feelings when they curve downwards. Pinched lips demonstrate a refusal to take something in – during a negotiation, this signals a resistance towards new ideas presented by the other party.

What does it mean when a negotiator touches his nose? The nose is one of the final "authorities" in our body. Figuratively speaking, we check with it regarding whether something is good for us or not. When someone names a price during a negotiation, for example, and touches his nose in the process, he is afraid that the price might be too high. In a sense, touching one's nose is a sign of critical examination and reflection.

We are often unable to control our facial expressions – however, it is not necessary to do so. Most people are reluctant to rehearse particular facial expressions solely for the purpose of increasing their influence on others. They want to further the negotiation, to inform or persuade the other party – not to be an actor! But there are things that one can do to simply come across as friendly. Keep an open and sympathetic look about you. A friendly, smiling face can work wonders even before a word is spoken, even when dealing with "neutral" matters. A smile springs from a sense of well-being and always corresponds to positive vibes. Consider the following points when you negotiate:

- *Avoid sheepish smiles*
  The eyes of shy negotiators seem quizzical, and their smiles never seem complete.

- *Avoid ironic smiles*
  The contours of one's eyes are different when one smiles ironically – the eyes narrow slightly, and an eyebrow is sometimes raised.

- *Avoid fake smiles*
  Put-on smiles do not look authentic. People often show too much teeth – and their eyes do not smile along.

- *Avoid cold smiles*
  When one smiles coldly, his eyes do not smile along. He usually keeps his head straight and his gaze fixed on his counterpart. Such a smile makes it seem like the person is looking forward to a personal triumph.

Natural tool #4: The neck

The neck is what makes it possible for us to move our heads. Negotiators whose necks move a lot are open to everything – they see not only what they know, but also what is new and unfamiliar. Some negotiators can be seen holding their necks in an erect, almost stiff, manner – they are signaling, "I mean what I say." People who hold their necks forward, as if on constant alert, will stick to their goals – anything to the left or right is just a distraction. In many cultures, this posture is considered a sign of reliability, although others criticize it as a reflection of narrow-mindedness. For those with this posture, evading, conceding, and making compromises are regarded adversely. If your counterpart's neck stiffens in the middle of a negotiation, then you can be sure that you've found a weak point in his argument. If he releases the tension and tilts his head, then that means you've brought him towards you – a slight tilt of the head shows a willingness to avoid direct confrontation. And a tilt of the head also expresses understanding, which makes it easier for one's counterpart to admit to mistakes or problems.

If your counterpart lays his hand on his neck, it means that he is trying to cover up some weakness – perhaps he does not know exactly how to respond or how to express his argument.

Natural tool #5: The chest as an energy reservoir

The chest houses the heart and lungs – our energy reservoirs. When you breathe deeply, your lungs are filled with oxygen – giving you more energy and making you look more alive. Your voice becomes stronger;

your shoulders loosen up. This relaxed posture, in turn, facilitates the free flow of your breathing and makes it easier for you to move about and take action.

Shallow breathing, on the other hand, suggests insecurity. It reduces tautness, creating the negative appearance of a sunken upper body. A paucity of oxygen makes one's voice noticeably weaker and uncertain. One's shoulders and arms drop, and arm movements become sparser – the chest must be open in order for one to make broader movements with one's arms. This inevitably gives others the impression of a lack of energy.

In the course of a negotiation, anything that instills doubt, introduces uncertainty, or requires a decision to be made will cause one to momentarily hold one's breath. If your counterpart continues to breathe normally when you make a proposal, then your message has not had its desired effect. If he holds his breath for a brief moment, this means that he is considering what you have said – he is taking a pause to decide whether he will accept your proposal or not.

Natural tool #6: The abdominal region

The more openly a negotiator displays his midsection, the more confident he appears. Facing his opponent with his abdominal region unprotected, he gives off a self-confident and fearless air. On the other hand, if his midsection is protected by crossed arms, and thus closed off from others, this represents a barrier that makes it more difficult for the other to trust him.

If you want to face your counterpart with confidence, then turn your body, and more specifically your midsection, towards him. This can foster feelings of closeness. The closer your counterpart comes towards you, the more trust he is expressing – and the more trust he will expect from you in return. However, if you get the feeling that he is getting *too* close, then he is probably trying to use territorial gains to establish dominance, as well as compel you to like and trust him – instead of simply trying to persuade you on the basis of his arguments alone. When attention is too intrusive, we start to find it unpleasant.

Natural tool #7: The shoulders and back

When one's shoulders are held straight, this signals that he has nothing weighing him down – neither physically nor mentally. Any burdens that we carry suppress our shoulders and curve our back. And when we are threatened by some danger, we instinctively pull in our head and lift our shoulders. In the context of negotiations, although we carry no literal burdens, we do bear symbolic ones, i.e., our responsibilities. In the course of your negotiations, you have undoubtedly heard lines like "I bear the responsibility for…" When someone bears a burden, their maneuverability is limited – and this is the case in negotiations as well.

And what is your counterpart saying when he gives you the "cold shoulder"? Turning one's shoulder towards another, instead of facing him with one's body, implies rejection. A cold shoulder is always an inflexible shoulder – the arm attached to it can neither give nor take anything. Trying to negotiate across a cold shoulder is like trying to negotiate across a wall, and there will be no flexibility at all from the other side.

Natural tool #8: The arms and hands

You have undoubtedly noticed that everyone constantly uses their arms and hands while negotiating. You wonder what it means when your boss repeatedly "stabs" his pen in your direction, or why your new coworker's knuckles get so white when he presents his new ideas. A negotiation can truly seem like a theater play. But what's behind all these gestures?

Negotiators use conscious and subconscious movements of their arms and hands to bolster the words they are saying. At the same time, one's gestures always reflect one's inner stance as well. Several different kinds of gestures can be distinguished:

- *Symmetrical gestures*
  These come across as stiff and boring over the long run. Fortunately, most people's movements and gestures are spontaneous. If, however, a negotiator continuously moves his arms and hands in a precisely symmetrical manner – i.e., always moving both sides exactly the same – it quickly starts to look

unnatural and monotonous. Symmetrical gestures are also often small gestures and can reflect narrow-mindedness.

- *Asymmetrical gestures*
  These come across as natural and loose – whether one hand or both are in motion, they're not doing exactly the same thing. One hand might gesticulate while the other comes to a rest. It doesn't matter whether it's conscious or subconscious. Most people have a "strong" hand and a "weak" hand – the strong hand is more expressive than the weak hand. When you speak with a piece of paper in your hand, try to hold it in your weak hand so that your strong hand is free to express itself with gestures.

- *Functional gestures*
  Our hands "punctuate" the things we are saying at any given moment. This can happen consciously or subconsciously. You may point in the direction of a person whom you are mentioning, for example. Or you may "show" what you are saying via concrete movements – e.g., counting off one-two-three points on your fingers, waving off some idea you disagree with, etc.

Vibrant gestures are an asset! A negotiator basically appears "open" when his arms and hands move freely away from his body, instead of being used to shield himself or barricade himself off. Gestures look natural when they are not narrowly confined to the wrist, but rather start from the elbow – or, for some people, even from the shoulder. Small, narrow gestures can seem repressed. One's gestures should use only one's upper body – anything below the belt can be awkward. And to the extent possible, one's movements should not be fast, frantic, or jerky, but rather calm and harmonious.

The three sorts of basic hand motions described below are also meaningful – namely palm-down hand motions, open hand motions, and dominant hand motions. Each and every person makes use of all three – although one or the other will predominate, depending upon the person's nature.

Palm-down hand motions
When a party to a negotiation shows only the backs of his hands, he thus hides the more delicate palm area. His counterpart will not be able to shake the feeling that this person has something else to hide as well. Even if he places both hands on the table face-down and promises that he is making an excellent offer, his counterpart will still believe that he is holding something back.

Open hand motions
By contrast, when a negotiator gestures with his hands open, he shows his palms. This signals: "I'm showing you what I hold in my hands. I've got nothing to hide." His counterpart feels like he is ready to share and reach compromises, rather than trying to take anything away. Open hands naturally tend to move upwards, as well as side-to-side; we associate these motions with self-confidence and generosity. Giving something with an open hand means not imposing anything upon the other – as if one were presenting one's offer on a platter. The other party can choose whether or not he wants to accept it. When one makes an open offer, one should made sure to leave one's hands open for at least two seconds, so that the other party has time to "grasp" it. Imagine if someone were to offer you a piece of cake on a platter, and then immediately yank the platter away from you – you

would presume that the offer was not serious. Quick movements have a hint of aggressiveness and hide a fear of rejection – but someone who really stands behind his offer has no reason to fear rejection. Another advantage of having one's hand open is that it prevents the dominant index-finger effect, thus avoiding any risk of patronizing of one's counterpart. The more open gestures you get into the habit of making, the more positive effects this will have.

Dominant hand motions
Dominant hand motions exercise pressure. They move downwards, with a suppressive effect. Behind any such gesture lies a desire to prevail over the other – against the other's will, if necessary. Negotiators who want to dominate rarely have positive impacts.

The following checklist can help you translate some common gestures that you will encounter repeatedly over the course of your negotiations.

What does it mean? Common gestures and their meanings	
Reaching out into the other party's space – even more dominant when done with the index finger extended:	This is based on a need to demonstrate superiority. It usually generates a negative reaction from the other party – they instinctively either shrink away or go on the counterattack.
Picking up a document, turning towards the other party, and highlighting certain points with one's hand open:	A positive way to present an offer to the other party. Both sides can consider the offer simultaneously and work on the matter together.
Holding something up in front of the other party's nose:	A way to create a wall between oneself and one's counterpart. An open laptop or briefcase has the same effect – the other side will feel like you have something to hide.

Building barriers with pens:	Negotiators put up barriers when they feel threatened. These barriers can include arms, papers, or pens – anything one puts between oneself and one's counterpart. And even if the barrier is something as small as a pen, it still obstructs communication.
Putting one's hands together and drumming one's fingertips against each other:	The fingertips are seeking new points of contact between the person's expectations and the actual offer on the table. "Does it fit the bill – or do I need something more?
Placing one's index fingers and thumbs together in a "double pistol":	The extended thumbs show a desire for dominance, while the know-it-all index fingers signal the forthcoming "shot".
Placing one's hand against one's mouth:	With this gesture, the negotiator is forcing himself to keep quiet and let the other side speak – even if he already knows the answer.
Clasping one's hands together and then splaying out the fingers:	This is a defense mechanism, like the quills of a porcupine. The negotiator does not want to take anything in – and it would be impossible for him to accept anything with his hands in this position.

Natural tool #9: The legs and feet

In any negotiation, one wants to take a firm stance. Consider this vivid image – sumo wrestlers, for example, need to take a firm stance, keeping as much contact with the ground as possible in order to avoid being pummeled out of the ring by their opponent. Likewise, a negotiator who wants to defend his position as strongly as possible should stand firmly on the ground. Make sure to distribute your weight evenly between your feet.

You can't make progress if you're not moving forward – so many negotiators pace around the conference room while they negotiate. This movement also helps keep their minds moving forward as they think through problems or devise new ideas.

While sitting, your feet can leave the ground more easily than while standing or walking around. When someone is said to have "both feet on the ground", it means that he is realistic – and this is also reflected when a person literally keeps both feet on the ground, even while seated. Removing one's feet from the ground signifies distancing oneself from reality, not wanting to deal with it right now.

When you negotiate while seated, as is usually the case, there will not be any major problems with your stance. Sit in a relaxed and easy manner, with your legs not curled back up beneath the chair (nor crossed when in conservative circles), but rather simply standing on the floor beside each other. Samy Molcho recommends making full use of the surface of your chair. A person who sits on the edge of his chair seems uncertain – as if he feels like the seat is not fully his, or as if he were about to leave.

The movements of your upper body are dependent upon your sitting position. If your feet are extended too far forward, then your upper body will automatically lean back – in which case it becomes more difficult to "move closer" to your counterpart. If your legs point straight down or are drawn back just slightly, then it becomes easier for you to move towards him.

Negotiators who stand or lean to the side while conversing are hedging, either rationally or emotionally. They are receptive, but don't want to take a clear stand. When your counterpart leans to the side, he may say things like, "I'll have to think about it" or "Interesting, we'll have to discuss this further". Try to get him to sit up straight – only then will he express himself clearly and purposefully.

Set the right tone – Using your voice correctly

"In the right key one can say anything. In the wrong key, nothing: the only delicate part is the establishment of the key." This quote from George Bernard Shaw is especially applicable to negotiations. Your voice goes straight to your counterpart's gut, immediately and unfiltered, penetrating it to create an opening for your words and their message. The tone of your voice is largely responsible for setting the tone of the discussion. It reveals your inner emotions – whether you're strong and confident or whether you're doubtful, insecure, bored, or unhappy. Your voice and your manner of speaking are gauges of your authenticity, conveying appreciation, interest, concern, warmth, or understanding. Anyone would rather listen to a negotiator with a mellifluous voice than a negotiator with an unpleasant voice – fortunately, though, almost any healthy voice sounds good when using proper speaking technique.

TIP:
Speak clearly! Modulate your voice! Speak in short, clear sentences with rising-then-falling intonation – this way, your voice always returns automatically to a lower pitch, which is better on your counterpart's ears.

Accents and dialects

Stick with your own regional accent or dialect; no accent or dialect is better or worse than any other. But there's a limit to the notion of "talking naturally" – if you notice that your accent or dialect is interfering with the discussion because your words are not actually being understood, then you should adopt a more neutral way of speaking.

Try to give the impression of common ground with your counterpart by adapting your speech patterns accordingly. The rule of thumb is to "speak to the situation". The more formal or official the context and your counterpart's speech, the more you should approximate this – though always without sounding artificial. On the other hand, the more informal or casual a situation is, the more colloquially you can speak.

CASE STUDY: REHEARSING AT THE CAFÉ

Noah meets up with his sister Nellie at a café. He tells her about how frustrated he is by the bank's denial of his loan application. "I've got such a great business idea – why don't they understand? Can you give me some tips for next time?" Nellie is flattered that her brother has asked her. She has him describe his conversation with the loan officer in detail; she then gives him some feedback, describing both what he did well and what he could improve. Then she suggests that he do a dry run with her for practice. She will play the role of the loan officer.

NELLIE: Mr. Nelson, why exactly do you need a loan of $20,000?

NOAH: I need the $20,000 for my business start-up costs. I'm a design engineer, so I need a powerful computer. My future clients are from the automotive industry, and I'll need a variety of different professional software packages, depending on the client – in other words, I'll need three different programs for Ford, Chrysler, and GM. The majority of the loan is needed for technical set-up costs. The rest is for the company website and logo design." (*Noah looks Nellie in the eye as he speaks in a loud, firm voice.*)

NELLIE: I see – that sounds reasonable. But I'd like you to explain more about the services that you plan to offer – you said you'll be working as a design engineer for different automobile companies?

NOAH: (*smiles, with his body straight and taut*) I'd be glad to explain. (*pause, with eye contact*) The major automakers are always working on developing their vehicles – and they've outsourced many steps of the process in order to save money. Many of their projects are being handled by independent engineering companies these days. I'm confident that I can be successful in delivering such services as well.

NELLIE: Mr. Nelson, you are (*flips through his documents*) 28 years old. You're still quite young. And you just finished your studies last year.

NOAH: (*with a grin*) That's correct. But I actually trained as an auto mechanic after high school. Then I went on to study mechanical engineering at UCLA; I've also interned with Ford and I've got some good contacts there now. My clients will appreciate both my knowledge of the corporate side and my practical experience as an auto mechanic. I've got much more than just the degree.

NELLIE: (*raising her hand to high-five Noah*) Well, if the decision were mine, you'd get the loan... but better wear a suit next time!

Our voices are as distinctive as our fingerprints

Voice expert Eva Loschky tells about an experiment carried out at the Max Planck Institute in Leipzig, in which researchers deciphered the messages hidden within the sound of a person's voice. When we first meet someone with whom we will negotiate, neurobiological responses are automatically triggered inside us – the person's eyes, voice, manner of speaking, facial expression, and body movements provoke an entire range of reactions. Our counterpart's external signals are activated within our own bodies by the corresponding neurons. By sensing other people's emotions inside our own selves, we gain an instantaneous, intuitive understanding of what moves them.

Our brains store these experiences as what researchers call "somatic markers". Your counterpart's nonverbal presence either inspires you with confidence or strikes you as unfriendly and untrustworthy. The corresponding bodily reactions are stored within you, in connection with that person – and whenever you think of that person in the future, the exact same bodily reactions are activated again.

In negotiations, your voice and demeanor have an effect on your counterpart within the first three seconds – even before he registers and processes your actual words. According to researchers who study decision-making and analyze the significance of empirical knowledge, one can think of the mind's adaptive unconscious as a sort of "supercomputer", which quickly and imperceptibly processes the vast quantities of data that a person is constantly taking in.

How your gut helps your brain – Intuition in negotiations

The increasingly fast-paced and complex nature of negotiation has made intuitive decision-making ever more important. According to the most recent psychological and neurological studies, intuitive decision-making is more efficient – and often yields better decisions – than the much-vaunted deliberative decision-making process.

Gut decisions

Psychologist Gerd Gigerenzer became well-known through his book *Gut Feelings*, which has been published in six languages and gives many examples to illustrate how such decisions work. Managers always say that they must proceed as rationally as possible when they make decisions, listing out all the pros and cons and weighing them accordingly – and this may sound logical, but it presumes that the human mind works like a calculator. For Gigerenzer, logic is just one of the tools that comprise intelligence. According to him, we usually decide things intuitively by relying on gut feelings that are the product of simple rules of thumb – of which we are often not even conscious. Still, writes Gigerenzer, these intuitive decisions are not only more efficient and faster, but are often simply better.

When proceeding intuitively, a negotiator invariably makes his decision on the basis of a single good reason. In an experiment at New York University, students were asked to guess the winner of a random selection of games from the 1996-97 National Basketball Association season, knowing only the halftime score and the number of games each team won during the season. The students guessed correctly 78% of the time. According to Gigerenzer, these results were incredible: "We had long known that people often follow a 'take-the-best' strategy, but had treated this as an irrational behavior that arose from certain cognitive limitations. Now, for the first time, we had evidence that a simple rule of thumb could work just as well as an exact calculation of probabilities."

The truly amazing thing was that the rate of success was actually improved by having less information. "Good information must ignore information. This improves quality," says Gigerenzer. The apparent paradox can be explained by the fact that not all information is actually relevant. The art of good prediction lies in extracting the data that really matters – and leaving aside all the rest. It is exactly this strategy that is embodied by the "take-the-best" strategy.

The fact that it is difficult for us to grasp this notion, according to Gigerenzer, lies in the fact that we have all internalized the supposed ideal that says, "More information is always better. More time is always better. More choice is always better. More calculations are always better." These notions are deeply ingrained within us, but they are wrong, he says. Intuition itself does not need to be "trained" in the true sense of the word – it is innate and is a basic function of our brains. However, we have been taught otherwise in school. In any case – we decide particularly well when we don't think about things. For both chess players and athletes, the first move the player considers has been proven to be the best in most instances. And experiments have shown that even in the case of choosing an apartment, the results are better when time is limited and an intuitive course of action is necessary.

So: trust your intuition! Listen to your gut and have confidence in it – or at the very least, treat it a valuable advisor during the course of your negotiations!

How to use intuition in your negotiations

- If you rely on intuitive decisions, then make sure you have enough knowledge and experience on which to base them. Your subconscious "advisor" can only analyze data that it has previously taken in.
- Tune out for a bit after a complex negotiation. Go for a walk or take a nap – let your unconscious mind go to work for you. Many good ideas come while in the shower.
- Trust in your unconscious mind to deliver good solutions; bear with the uncertainty.
- Listen to what your body is saying. Somatic markers present themselves dependably. Something may be a "load on your shoulders" or a "pain in the neck". It is helpful to play through

various scenarios in your mind and pay attention to how they make you feel.
- Intuitive decisions often need to be rationally analyzed and justified in order for them to gain acceptance in the business environment.

CASE STUDY: HOW THE GUT HELPS THE HEAD SOLVE PROBLEMS

Fleur's boss, Tom, has told her that he will give her some important background information for her negotiations with a new Italian client. Five times he has scheduled a meeting to discuss this information with her – and each time, he has popped into her office fifteen minutes before the scheduled meeting to postpone it.

Without Tom's information, Fleur and Nellie are unable to prepare for the client's product launch. The entire team is fed up with meeting postponements by now. Fleur feels helpless. She is disappointed in Tom and angry about him leaving her in the lurch. She wants to find some new way of working with him – but at the moment, she has no idea how.

Then she remembers that, many years ago, her mentor had given her an envelope with the words, "*When you get stuck and have no idea what else to do – open this envelope!*" written on it. He had said, "My own mentor gave it to me many years ago. Maybe someday you'll pass it on to someone else too." Then he had laughed, reiterating that she should only open the envelope when she truly needed it.

Fleur now opens the envelope and unfolds the sheet of paper inside it. It reads as follows:

Eight steps to mental intuition

- Find a place where you are comfortable, so that you can achieve clarity and calm.
- Write down the issue or problem that you want to solve.
- Go into a meditative state, letting go of your thoughts and feelings. Just relax.
- In order to achieve clarity, place your doubting, analytical mind into an imaginary box on the ground.
- Relax consciously, making sure that you are breathing calmly. Focus on your inner center, drawing your point of focus upwards to the top of your head.
- Take as much time as you need. Let your thoughts drift in a wide-open space of intuition.
- When you're ready, leave this space, letting an old vessel bring you back. Return your point of focus to the center of your chest, and take a few deep breaths. Remove your mind from the imaginary box on the ground, open your eyes, and write down everything you sensed in the wide-open space of intuition.
- Do not be surprised if your intuition continues to reverberate and brings you further ideas over the course of the following days.

Fleur was skeptical at the start, but tried it out. She felt extraordinarily fresh and clear. A good idea came to her: She will plan to have lunch with Tom once a week, and then get together with him for a meeting immediately afterwards. That evening, she calls up her mentor. "At first I thought it was just esoteric junk. But looking back, I think it works."

"That's great, Fleur," says her mentor. "Not all intuition is the same. Research says that we access our inner voices in two ways: emotionally – the classic gut feeling – and mentally – the inspiration from above that suddenly sparks an idea. Good thinkers can access their thoughts without feeling emotionally drawn towards them nor repulsed by them. Take advantage of this in your future negotiations – it has always helped me reach solutions with intuition and reason."

Three classic negotiation scenarios

To close this chapter, we will take a closer look at three classic negotiation scenarios:

- Territoriality at the negotiating table
- Greetings that get you started on the right track
- The seating arrangement as a reflection of the power structure

Scenario 1: Territoriality – Of dominance and subordination

Human social behavior manifests itself in every negotiation. Social signals announce each person's status in the hierarchy and his role on the team. Social status is reflected in one's body language. The more relaxed and openly a negotiator moves about and the more he takes advantage of his freedom of movement, the more clearly this indicates a lack of fear. What are some nonverbal attributes of strong people? One important signal is that the person makes calm movements that occupy lots of space. Dominant signals go downwards, from above to below – a strong person places his hand on the other's shoulder, or stops the other person by placing his hand on the other's arm. If a person decides when the negotiations are over, this is also a sign of his superiority. A person who wants to take the lead must see his goals clearly before him, so a clear gaze is a signal of power as well. The powerful person's movements are efficient and express their meaning clearly – on the other hand, when someone is indecisive and feels torn apart, his body signals this with its inconsistent movements.

Scenario 2: Greeting the other party

How you greet your counterpart will set the negotiations on their course. The classic greeting ritual in most of the English-speaking business world involves the participants going directly up to one another, standing face-to-face, and greeting each other with a firm handshake. This is how it is done when two people of equal power meet at eye level, forgoing conflict. A confident negotiator may stretch out his arm towards his counterpart even while still walking towards him – this person is a go-getter.

Watch out for the following mistakes when you enter others' offices:

- *Don't hang out in the doorway.*
  This sends a signal of uncertainty.

- *Don't hang out in the center of the room.*
  This is a sign of meek respect.

- *Also, don't hang out in the center of the room and stick your arm out from there to greet your counterpart.*
  This will force him into an uncomfortable position.

- *Don't place your briefcase in your counterpart's spot.*
  This is an infringement of his territory. The negotiating table is basically like a big sandbox.

- *Don't build a wall between yourself and others with your briefcase.*
  This will give off the subconscious impression that you've got something to hide.

Scenario 3: Who sits where? – The seating arrangement

The seating arrangement also plays an important role in negotiations. The negotiating table can be seen as representing the object of the negotiation. The dominance of individual parties can often be deduced based on how much room they take up. Confident parties occupy a large area of the negotiating table, with documents, pens, and other items spread out before them. The uncertain negotiator piles his papers up together neatly, sometimes even pulling them back off the edge of the table a bit. He may keep his hands below the table as well, only occasionally bringing them out to emphasize some point he is making.

The person leading the negotiations is often the one with the highest status; he sits at the head of the table. Others who know where they stand will sometimes try to demonstrate this in some way, setting themselves off from their team members.

One can often tell whether a negotiation is more competitive or cooperative by seeing whether the parties are sitting opposite each other confrontationally or whether they are sitting together at an angle that allows everyone to look at documents simultaneously. Round tables have been proven to work in difficult negotiations, stressing equality between the parties and making the hierarchy take a backseat.

SOLUTION TO SELF-ASSESSMENT 7.1

Noah is very nervous. This is normal at the start – requesting a loan from a bank is always a bit unsettling.

"Clothes make the man!" This notion is accurate to the extent that wearing formal business attire certainly affects a person's self-confidence. Someone who has never worn a tie would naturally feel uncomfortable the first time he puts one around his neck. There is no universal dress code for negotiations – the most important thing is that your clothing fit your own personal style. In this respect, Noah may have been right in sticking with his jeans; it is also possible, however, that he may have felt more comfortable in a suit.

Noah speaks in a confusing, somewhat incoherent manner. His speech is too unstructured and colloquial. Together with his scratching and fidgeting, this makes him seem unsteady.

Noah avoids direct eye contact. Pressing his hands against his thighs also makes him seem tense – and neither open nor self-confident. Gesturing more freely and openly would have been better.

Nodding affirmatively is a very good thing – but doing so too often can make a negotiator appear sycophantic.

It is perfectly okay to ask for a drink of water. But the whole train of thought that Noah delivers in the process would not be of interest to anyone.

The banker's follow-up questions show that Noah has not stated his key points clearly enough. He has gotten completely lost in the details.

One's materials also contribute to the overall impression that one makes. The banker is likely to draw conclusions regarding Noah's work from the collection of loose papers he is carrying around.

SUMMARY: BODY LANGUAGE AND INTUITION

▶ Why is body language so important in negotiations?

Think about how much your own body language says about your mindset. You always carry your "natural tools" – your facial expressions, gestures, and posture – with you, wherever you go. Nonverbal signals are always more powerful than the spoken word. Learn to pay attention to your counterpart's body language – you can figure out a lot about his attitude and emotional state.

▶ **Should one interpret individual signals or the language of the entire body?**

Do not interpret the natural tool of individual body parts in isolation from the rest of the body. Just like with a jigsaw puzzle, you have to put the individual pieces together to see the big picture – and to get to know your counterpart's overall mood. If you understand the meanings behind the nine most important natural tools of the human body, then this will give you a big advantage in your negotiations.

▶ **How can a negotiator's voice affect his negotiations?**

Our voices set the "tone" of our negotiations, reflecting our internal moods. Tense situations can lead to impasses, so make a conscious effort to be relaxed at the negotiation table. When you are stressed, proper breathing can help reduce your tension.

▶ **Is intuition just something esoteric, or can gut decisions actually be useful in negotiations?**

The topic of intuition has been researched extensively in recent years. Gerd Gigerenzer's book *Gut Decisions* presents research explaining how our brain helps our gut make decisions. Stay in touch with your gut feelings, bringing them into play as an additional factor in your rational decision-making process.

I wish you, the reader, much success in your own negotiations to come. May "BETTER NEGOTIATING. THE TRAININGBOOK" truly serve you and your negotiation partners. All the best!

Jutta Portner
Munich, Germany
March 2017

Business Coaching | Managementtraining & Beratung
Seeuferstr. 59 | 82541 Ambach | Germany

+49 8177 / 99 85 458

welcome@c-to-be.de | www.c-to-be.de

BIBLIOGRAPHY

- Cialdini, Robert B.: Die Psychologie des Überzeugens. Huber/ Bern: 2005
- Donaldson, Michael C. und Donaldson, Mimi: Negotiating for Dummies. John Wiley&Sons/Foster City, USA: 1996
- Edmüller, Andreas und Wilhelm, Thomas: Argumentieren. Wrs/ Planegg: 1998
- Fisher, Roger und Ury, William: Getting to Yes. Random House/ London: 1999
- Fisher, Roger und Ury, William und Patton, Bruce: Das Harvard-Konzept. Der Klassiker der Verhandlungstechnik. Campus/ Frankfurt, New York: 2004
- Fisher, Roger und Shapiro, Daniel: beyond reason. Using Emotions as You Negotiate. Viking Penguin/New York, USA: 2005
- Gigerenzer, Gerd: Bauchentscheidungen. Bertelsmann/München: 2007
- Harter, Gitte: Erfolgreich verhandeln. Haufe/Planegg: 2006
- Karrass, Chester L.: The Negotiating Game. Harper Collins/New York, USA: 1992
- Karrass, Chester L.: In Business As In Life – You Don't Get What You Deserve, You Get What You Negotiate. Stanford Street Press/ Los Angeles, USA: 1996
- Kennedy, Gavin: Everything is NEGOTIABLE – How to get the Best Deal Everytime. Arrow Books/London: 1997
- Kennedy, Gavin: Essential Negotiation. Profile Books Ltd./ London: 2004
- Kunkel, Agnes und Bräutigam, Peter und Hatzelmann, Elmar: Verhandeln nach Drehbuch. Redline Wirtschaft/Heidelberg: 2006
- Lax, David A. und Sebenius, James K.: 3 D Negotiation. Harvard Business School Press/Boston, USA: 2006
- Levine, Robert: Die große Verführung. Psychologie der Manipulation. Piper/München: 2005

- Malhotra, Deepak und Bazerman, Max H.: Negotiation Genius. Harvard Business School. Bantam Books/New York, USA: 2007
- Mastenbroek, Willem: Verhandeln. Strategie. Taktik. Technik. Gabler/Wiesbaden: 1992
- Molcho, Samy: Körpersprache des Erfolgs. Heinrich Hugendubel/ München: 2005
- Nöllke, Matthias: Schlagfertigkeit. STS/Planegg: 1999
- Portner, Dieter: Überzeugend diskutieren. Beltz Verlag/ Weinheim: 2000
- Ruede-Wissmann, Wolf: Satanische Verhandlungskunst und wie man sich dagegen wehrt. Area/München: 1993
- Ury, William: Getting past No. Bantam/New York, USA: 1993

GABAL global

English Editions by GABAL Publishing

Who We Are

GABAL provides proven practical knowledge and publishes media products on the topics of business, success, and life. With over 600 experienced, international authors from various industries and education, we inspire businesses and people to move forward.

GABAL. Your publisher.
Motivating. Sympathetic. Pragmatic.

These three adjectives describe the core brand of GABAL. They describe how we think, feel, and work. They describe the style and mission of our books and media. GABAL is your publisher, because we want to bring you forward. Not with finger-pointing, not divorced from reality, not pointy-headed or purely academic, but motivating in effect, sympathetic in appearance, and pragmatically-oriented toward results.

Our books have only one concern: they want to help the reader improve. In business. For success. In life.

Our target reader
People who want to develop personally and/or professionally

As a modern media house GABAL publishes books, audio books, and e-books for people and companies that want to develop further. Our books are aimed at people who are looking for knowledge about current issues in business and education that can be put into practice quickly.

For more information, see the GABAL global website:

http://www.iuniverse.com/Packages/GABAL-Global-Editions.aspx

Printed in the United States
By Bookmasters